The Orkney Chronicles

by Anne Buxton and Jacqueline McEwan

THE ORKNEY CHRONICLES
1900 & 1989

The Jamieson Library, Newmill , 1992

First published in 1992 in paperbound format for the Jamieson Library of Women's History, Newmill, Penzance, Cornwall TR20 4XN by the Patten Press, 66 Hayle Terrace, Hayle, Cornwall, TR27 4BT.

ISBN 1 872229 03 4

Cover and detail design: Carole Page
Photographic reproduction: Bob Berry

Typeset at The Patten Press
Printed and bound by Billings of Worcester

Table of contents

List of Illustrations

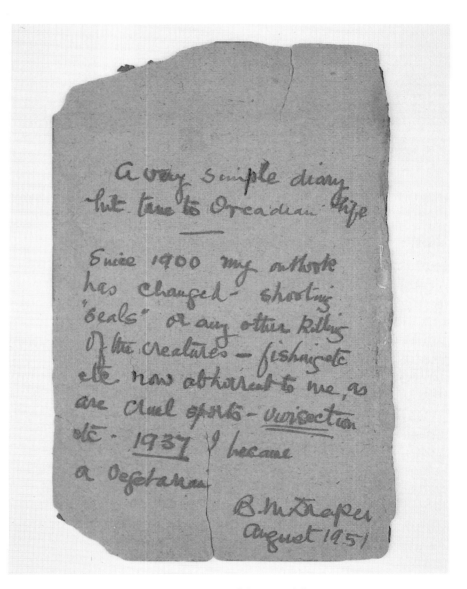

1. Inside the front cover of the tattered diary.

PROLOGUE

It was our friend, Alan Green, who first found the diary which was to become this journey of discovery. He purchased the small, tattered notebook for a pound in a secondhand bookshop in Gloucestershire, not being able to resist the close, neat script which announced its purpose: A Trip to Orkney, June, 1900. After reading it, Alan thought this lone turn-of-century traveller might provide us with an intrigue, and his assessment could not have been more accurate.

Inside the front cover, an enticing note gave us our first clues about the author.

"A very simple diary but true to Orcadian life
Since 1900 my outlook has changed - shooting seals or any other killing   of the creatures, fishing, etc. now abhorrent to me, as are cruel sports....
In 1937 became a vegetarian.
B.M. Draper, August, 1951."

From the pages another story unfolded. A young woman, seemingly travelling alone - despite the 'we' and 'us' of her diary entries - had visited the tiny Orcadian island of Flotta from her home in Brechin. By train from Aberdeen, she observed the varied beauties of the Scottish countryside prior to arrival at Thurso, where a succession of boats - steamer, packet, rowing boat - took her to Flotta, the Manse, the church by the bay, the night sky, puffins and seals, the annual sheep shearing, fishing trips at midnight, visiting the poor and sick in their smoky one-roomed cottages.....

Quite independently, both of us (the 'readers' of this 'very simple diary') began to dream of following in the traveller's steps. When we shared these thoughts, it was with enormous excitement that we set about planning our adventure.

So, where is Flotta? Is it still inhabited? So many small islands have become depopulated, that what was in 1900 a thriving community might now be a forgotten landscape.

We wrote to 'The Occupier, The Manse, Flotta, Orkney' not confident of receiving a reply. Briefly outlining the diary's contents, we indicated our enthusiasm and our desire to visit Flotta to retrace the young woman's footsteps. Writing to the Manse seemed the logical first step in our research, and was the present owner able to tell us anything of its history and previous occupants?

We consulted the Ordnance Survey map, only to discover a considerable area of Flotta now housing a vast oil terminal. At least the island would still be inhabited - but how changed from the community and landscape of 1900? Would any trace remain?

A delightful letter arrived in reply from the Manse. Phyllis Sinclair, the present owner, wrote warmly with as much detail as she could give. Built in 1892 the house, latterly no longer used as a Manse, had fallen into total disrepair. She had purchased it some three years previously from the Church of Scotland, renovated it, and finally moved in during the summer of 1988. She was able to tell us that the eldest child of the Minister and his wife, Mr. and Mrs. Mitchell of the diary, who was born in the Manse in September, 1900, is still living on Flotta. Mary Fortnum had been told of our intentions, was looking forward to meeting us and reading the diary. Now, the whole story was beginning to focus, and our 89 year gap was closing like a fan.

Phyllis sent a photograph of Flotta, with the Manse in the distance nestling on the edge of Kirk Bay, a beautiful situation. Most prized of all, however, was her invitation to stay with her on our visit. Thus we would enjoy the special experience of being in the house where the diary was written and looking out of the same windows.

£1   June 13th 1913

"A Trip to the Orkney Islands"

Wednesday 17th June left Brechin with
the 2.5 train for Aberdeen, reaching
there about 4 o'clock. We went straight
to Benson's Temperance Hotel, and after
taking our wraps to the bedrooms and
freshening ourselves up after our journey
we had a walk through the principal
streets of the "Granite City". Between five
and six we spent some time in the
market, and went back to the hotel
in time for tea (with "Finnan Haddies")
which was served at 6-30. In the
evening we went to the Palace Theatre
and enjoyed the entertainment very
much. There were ponies and dogs,
monkeys and a goat and they all
performed particularly well. It was
a very sultry night and although
we were in bed by 10-30 sleep

2. First page of Miss Murray's diary

CHRONICLE I

A Trip to the Orkney Islands
June 13th 1900

Wednesday, 17 June left Brechin with the 2.5 for Aberdeen, reaching there about 4 o'clock. We went straight to Benson's Temperance Hotel, and after taking our wraps to the bedrooms and freshening ourselves up after our journey we had a walk through the principal streets of the "Granite City". Between five and six we spent some time in the market, and we went back to the hotel in time for tea (with "Finnan Haddies") which was served at 6.30. In the evening we went to the Palace Theatre and enjoyed the entertainment very much. There were ponies and dogs, monkeys and a goat, and they all performed particularly well. It was a very sultry night and although we were in bed by 10.30 sleep was not long in visiting us. At five next morning we were called and had an early breakfast. We left Aberdeen with the 6 o'clock train and passed through a very open country until Oyne was reached where several wooded hills stood out in bold relief against the sky. Huntly is a very pretty place, with trees in abundance.

A good many fine buildings stand on the outskirts of the town. Portsoy on the coast route is a lovely little place, as is also Cullen. The latter resembles Stonehaven very much with its pier on the right hand, and rocks at either side, forming a bay. One rocky point is very like Downie. Buckie, also on the coast has a fine light-house. On the approach to Fochabers lies a large tract of country all aflame with gorse. Patches of heather also were to be seen, and the bright yellow bloom made a fine contrast with the dark heather, not yet in flower. We made a longer stop at Elgin, which is a very fashionable place with a great many large houses. A few miles out from Elgin are the ruins of Pluscarden Abbey, an old Roman Catholic edifice. Near Forres one gets a splendid view of "Nelson Monument?" Clunie Hill Hydropathic is near Forres also. We passed the Spey, one of the fastest running rivers in Scotland. It is a splendid salmon river. The bed is very shallow, and the river overflows its banks often very suddenly. The train ran by the side of the estate of Brodie of Brodie. We saw some beautiful shrubs of Rhododendron in full bloom. On the approach to Nairn, on one side the country was richly wooded, and on the other the land was open with the sea beyond. After passing Nairn we saw a lot of cotton growing on a tract of heathery ground. Culloden lies two or three miles away on one side, near a new railway. We got a view of Ben Wyvis near Inverness, with the snow still on it. The Moray Firth lies between the railway and the hills. We caught a glimpse of Fortrose in Ross-shire. The Firth looks lovely in the sunshine, with the hills in the background. Inverness reached we had a cup of tea in the restaurant, the waiter was a German. The train for Thurso left at 9.50. We saw the Caledonian Canal, and a training ship lying in it, then the mouth of the Ness, and Cromarty lying to the north. The main road to Inverness ran for some time alongside the railroad, it was lined with trees. A peninsula, called the Black Isle lies between the Moray and Cromarty Firths, an immense piece of wooded land, thick with Scotch Firs. Hereabouts the country was brightened with the bright yellow of the mustard seed amongst the oats. Clumps of the wild Purple Iris were in flower by the side of the Beauly. At Dingwall where the train stopped a little our carriage was opposite the shop of Wlm Brown, Fruiterer & Florist. The line to "Strathpeffer" was on the right hand side (a distance of about 8 miles).

The line continues and goes over to the other side of Ross-shire whence one can get aboard the steamer, and sail "Over the sea to Skye."

3. Strath Fleet, from the train

Note: At Aberdeen we saw the result of a train accident, three men had been injured. The Cromarty Firth looked charming with the sunshine sparkling on its rippling waters, and a variegated fringe of thickly foliaged trees in their spring garb. A short stop at Novar, also at Invergordon, the latter is famed for its potatoes. Here we got a view of the mouth of the Cromarty and its two headlands. One of the fields we passed was white with a flock of gulls. A stop at Kildary and at Fearn. A herd of splendid Highland Cattle was in a field nearby. At 11.30 we came to Tain which lies at the mouth of the Dornoch Firth. Across the firth lies Dornoch, also Skiro Castle the residence of Andrew Carnegie, the millionaire, and far in the distance the Sutherland hills. The railway here goes through part of the Firth, in which lie two islands, hilly and clad with Scotch firs. There are several saw-mills scattered near the forests. A luxurious growth of broom intermingled with the silvery birches presented a charming scene. At Bonar Bridge Station we partook of delightful plates of pea soup, also tongue sandwiches with fine keen mustard. We saw a shooting-lodge lying at the foot of a forest-clad hill on the banks of the firth. Short stop at Culrain then Invershin. The river Shin wends its way through a lovely piece of country. We got but a glimpse of a wild gully in a bend of the river which here becomes narrower and more turbulent. The scene is a very romantic one. Passing through a deeply wooded valley in the Duke of Sutherland's property, the eye is delighted by the rowan and lime trees, and the graceful birch. Near Lairg, pronounced "Lai-rig" there are splendid sheep pastures with pretty little crofts scattered everywhere. Wooded parts get scarcer and scarcer. Stop at Rogart. The Mound formed of earth across the firth, and built up into a beautiful smooth road, is protected on either side by well-kept fences. Near it on the right are several bold rocky promontaries. The view of the firth from the Mound must be superb. On the summit of a woody hill stands the Monument erected to the memory of the present Duke of Sutherland's grandfather. From the distance it does not appear to be of very great height but it is said that one would find it impossible to throw a stone over it, standing at its base. The shoes are said to be six feet long. Golspie and Dunrobin. We got several passing glimpses of the Castle, a most magnificent building. "Towers and battlements it sees, bosomed high in tufted trees." The gardens lie at the back between the Castle and the firth. On the left hand side, another monument stands to the memory of the Duke's father. The estate is one of the wealthiest in Scotland. Then we came to the sea with a distant view of Tarbat Ness and the lighthouse. Brora has very wide streets, and the river flows through it. It has a beautiful large hotel, all ornamented with square pieces of red sandstone. Far in the distance the sea was of a deep deep blue, fading as it came nearer into a delicate tint of grey, sparkling in the sunshine. On the sea shore grass bents and sand dunes, gorse and bracken at the foot of the hills, beauty almost unsurpassable (in its kind) on either side. Loth, a splendid agricultural district here, all the crofts sheltered from the North winds by the highlands. In the midst of a little grove stood a pretty manse, whilst higher up appeared the church. A flight of cormorants (or scarfs - which is the local name for them) settled on some rocks. At Helmsdale we drank a tumbler full of milk each, very refreshing after the close heat of the carriage; we also had a nice thick 'shortie'. We passed the river Helmsdale which flows through Kildonan Strath, where about twenty years ago gold was found. Here was a high bank of uncultivated ground covered with moss, trees and primroses (the last we saw were at Cruchinblae). This is on the borders of Caithness. The very high mountains on the right hand side remind one of Glenesk, one behind another, one of the highest had its summit shrouded in mist, which as we passed was lifting. Still in Kildonan Strath. About forty years ago the people were evicted, and their dwellings burned to the ground. The shooting lodges, of which there are a good many hereabouts, mostly belong to the Duke of Sutherland; one of them was built of wood, and slated over walls as well as roof, only the chimneys being of stone. The hill of the name of Morven is very high, and is seen from any part of Caithness. Stop at Kinbrace. Near Forsinard lies a fine loch, surrounded by stretches of grassy land, and with mountains on the far side; there is another smaller loch further on with an island in its midst, very pretty. In the wide stretch of country between Sutherlandshire and Caithness, vast, solitary and mountainous, there is not a tree to be seen until we enter Forsinard, the last stopping place in Sutherlandshire. A "whamp" flew over the moor as we passed. Then we entered Caithness, still the solitudes of nature, no habitations, the hills further in the distance; grass and heather flats as far as the eye could reach with pools of water here and there. Altnabreac is the first stopping place in Caithness. "Sir Tollemache Sinclair of Thurso Castle" possesses a large part of this country. Brawl Castle belongs to him. At Georgemas Junction we changed for Thurso. The first station at which the train stops is Hoy, which is but half a mile from Georgemas. In this district *there is a quarry, and all the boundaries between the fields are built of flagstones, which are got there. The Thurso river, although not much bigger than the Omick, is famous for salmon fishing. A lovely churchyard stands on the bank of the river, facing the railway. In front of it are four terraces of beautifully kept grass, with two long flights of steps leading up. Our train journey ended at Thurso, and after procuring a trap we drove with our luggage to Scrabster where we got on board the steamer "St. Ola". The sea was very calm, and we had a delightful cross-over. We sailed through the "Scrabster Roads", and from thence into the Pentland Firth. We passed Holborn Head, with its lighthouse and fog-horn, looking down from there, what an awesome sight it must be, sheer precipices, the rocks shelving down to the sea. We made the acquaintance of the "Free Kirk" Minister of Cullen aboard the steamer. An old relative of his, Mrs. Charles Ogilvie, died in Brechin. On nearing Flotta, we left the steamer and were rowed in a small boat to a "Packet", the latter conveyed us to Pan Hope, where we re-entered the small boat, and were rowed ashore. It had been a beautiful day, and the night was a good one. We walked to the Manse, leaving the heaviest of our luggage to be carted up by one of the men. After our long day we enjoyed the ham-and-egg supper which awaited us very much. After resting a short time, we had some piano and violin music, and then retired to rest and sleep.*

On Friday we were too tired to do very much, however after several hours music, and some correspondence, we walked down to the Church. It is a large building for the island, and holds 240. The whole population is about 500.

On Saturday the three of us, Mr. and Mrs. Mitchell and myself, started to walk to the Post Office. Mr. Mitchell left us about half way to call - pay a visit of condolence - on a family of the name of Simpson. The husband and father had died on the Sunday before and his son, who by his own efforts rose to be an assistant professor in Edinburgh University, had come north for his father's funeral. Mrs. Mitchell and I continued our way, stopping to get the newspapers at one of the shops on the shore of Pan Bay. The woman who came to the door asked us in to rest, and we accepted her invitation for a few minutes. The peat fire was burning on the open hearth, a very rare thing now-a-days excepting in parts like this. A little dog called Darkie was lying almost helpless on the floor near the fire. It had been very bad with bronchitis for long and did not look as if it would live very long. Then we went on to the Post Office, which is of a very primitive appearance, compared to those in the South. After tea Mr. Mitchell retired to the study to prepare his sermon for the morrow. We sewed and talked until bed-time.

Sunday foggy but fair. The service begins at twelve in the summer, and is the only one. The walls of the Church within are of a pale blue, and the windows which all look out on one side, have each a plant of geraniums in the sill. Below the pulpit, the precentor sits in a small closed in pew. In front of his seat stands the organ, which has a lovely drapery of crimson velvet embroidered with white silk flowers and green leaves. It is lined with soft white figured silk and was a gift to the Church. The service was a nice one, and the sermon preached on the text Hebrews XIII Ch. XIV v. "Here have we no continuing city, but we seek one to come" was appropriate to the death of Sutherland

Simpson, one of the parishioners. After service the Sunday School was held, and as three of the teachers were absent, I was asked to help, by taking one of the classes. I did so, and found the children exceedingly diligent, quick at answering, and most polite. The people on the island are beautiful speakers, original and quaint. Dinner at three o'clock, rest until tea-time, and then played a few hymns. After supper and the reading we all went a walk, leaving the Manse about ten we did not return until 11.30. Although the weather through the day had been foggy and unfavourable, the night proved most propitious. The sea view from the west shore was a lovely one. Two boats lay out in the bay, and the sky, radiant with the last light of the sun before it set, was tinting the smooth surface of the waters beautifully. A Sabbath evening, with its solemn hush, a sunset sky with its warm and matchless display of ever-varying colour, the ocean calm and serene, reflecting the beauty of the heavens. Far in the distance the hills of Hoy with their crowns of mist, slowly lifting, and to the right the Mainland, with the island of Graemsay lying between, softly yet clearly outlined against the glowing sky. Soon we had to retrace our steps, but regretfully did we turn our backs on the lovely scene. At midnight it was so clear that I was able to read at the dining-room window, a circumstance which reminds one of the land of the "Midnight Sun". When the clock struck the hour we went to bed, and just as I was falling asleep I noticed that it was dawning. We had passed the hour, the darkest hour, a dark that was but light.

Monday morning about three o'clock the sun burst forth, and my bedroom was flooded with a glory all the more appreciated on account of the dark, dull unsettled days that had gone before. A few little house duties that needed attention kept Mrs. Mitchell and me busy in the morning, but every now and then we went out of doors to enjoy for a moment the bright sunshine, and to get a glimpse of the sparkling sea. After dinner we rested with our knitting or our books. We took tea at 5 o'clock and then set out for the West Shore to meet the steamer. Mr. Mitchell walked to Flotta Calf to attend to two lambs, the mother had been found dead by some fishers on Saturday.

A stiff breeze was blowing but we enjoyed the walk. Soon we left the road and struck out across a moor, with white patches of cotton brightening its dark expanse. Here and there also in a marshy part would be the yellow king-cup, and several other flowers just as pretty though perhaps not quite so easily distinguished. On reaching Housca we awaited the arrival of the "Hoy Head", but about 6.15 we turned homewards having been assured that it would not come that night. By the time we saw the Manse walls again, we were tired and glad to be seated. Ten o'clock struck before Mr. Mitchell appeared, but he had been glad to find the lambs alive, and everything prospering well. (Received letter from home.)

4. Kirk Bay, Flotta

Tuesday, 19th June. A foggy day, no outing at all. We occupied our time with writing letters, knitting and with music. After tea a young fellow, by name James Sabieson came in, and after Mr. Mitchell and he had a chat we had some violin music. Mr. Sabieson played very well, and I danced "Shaw Trns" and "Gillie Callerm" to his accompaniment. Mr. Sabieson had been in London for two months, but not liking it had returned to Orkney and intended to get into the Civil Service.

Wednesday, 20th June. Weather still foggy, not quite so thick as Tuesday. About 9.30 I donned my waterproof and started with Mr. Mitchell for the Post Office where the steamer delivered goods and letters and also took communications from Flotta. On the way back Mr. Mitchell called at a large house standing off the road, and asked Dr. Hill to tea. The night passed pleasantly with music, chatting, a game or two at draughts and so on. After supper the Doctor departed and we sat and talked in the gloaming till bedtime.

Thursday, 21st. Mr. and Mrs. Mitchell and I walked down to the steamer. I posted a letter for home, and was glad to receive Mamma's second one. It broke down after dinner, so I brought my diary up to date. After tea the weather improved and the sky, although cloudy in some parts was very pretty, especially in the west. Mr. and Mrs. Mitchell worked in the garden, whilst I took my book out, and enjoyed a read in the open air. The sky betokened a better day on the morrow, and lovely indeed proved Friday, 22nd.

About 11.30 Mr. Mitchell started on a round of visits, the day being so fine I accompanied him, "to see life", as he said. We had a lovely walk across the moor to Housca where we saw Andrew Sutherland, whom Mr. Mitchell commissioned to build up a dike on Flotta Calf in preparation for the sheep shearing. We called in at several houses on our homeward way. In one house, or rather hovel, for indeed it looked a miserable place to dwell in, a poor old woman was lying in a close stuffed up box bed. We could scarcely get in the doorway was so short, and the room after we were in it would be impossible to describe. How the old couple (the husband was out) could exist in such an atmosphere I cannot tell. Both are over eighty years of age, and are on the Parish. Mr. Mitchell gave her some pecuniary assistance, and indeed appearances told it was needful. The poor creature crawled out of bed somehow, and groaning in a piteous voice, managed to reach an arm chair, by the smoky peat fire. We stayed but a minute, and glad indeed we were to be out once more in the open. We should indeed be thankful for our warm, airy comfortable homes, such a dwelling would arouse feelings of thankfulness in the hearts even of those in poverty, for within its walls was pictured not only poverty but beggarliness, pain and misery. We did not arrive at the Manse again until 2.30 and the dinner proved most acceptable after our long walk. The afternoon was a most favourable one, bright and sunshining, and I was tempted to go out of doors. Accordingly, I took Crocket's "Lilac Sunbonnet" with me, and sauntered for an hour or so over a breezy moor. About four o'clock Mr. and Mrs. Mitchell hailed me from a croft on the hill, and closing my book I went with them to pay other visits. One old woman who was in bed, was very glad to see the Minister. She was in a very nervous state, so before leaving Mr. Mitchell read a chapter and engaged in prayer. After tea a boy of about seventeen years of age came in to return some books Mr. Mitchell had lent him, and to get a few more. He talked away very smartly about his escapades with an old muzzle-loader. Dr. Hill also called but as Mr. Mitchell was out, he did not get the game of draughts he desired. After an hour or so had passed the Doctor rose to go, and Arthur Haye accompanied him. After Mr. Mitchell had returned, we all walked to the pillar to post some letters.

Saturday 23rd. The day dawned fair and gave promise of a delightful outing. We rose a little earlier, and had breakfast before getting together the necessaries for our expedition to Flotta Calf. About 10 o'clock we started for Pan Bay, carrying with us a large jar of porter. Jacobina and one of the company followed with the milk in two pails. On reaching the pier we got into a large flat-bottomed boat and were rowed to the Packet. Two or three boat loads had already been boarded, so shortly after we were settled comfortably, they set sail. We numbered about thirty altogether, men, women and boys. The sea was very calm, and the breeze did not spring up until we were a good bit on our way. Two of the boatsmen rowed for some time, but when the wind rose, the sails were spread. A radiant sky, a glorious sunshine, a lucid expanse of ocean stretching far in the distance to the left, part of Flotta lying pleasantly outlined against the horizon, and we sailed on in the midst of nature, beautiful and serene. We rounded Rone Head, and entered the Sound which flows between Flotta and the Calf. Soon we had to re-enter the smaller boat, and were rowed ashore. Mrs. Mitchell and I climbed the rocky bank, and seated ourselves in a niche near the edge where we had a splendid view of the shearers at their work. Mr. Mitchell and one or two others started with the boys to chase the sheep round to the path which we had previously climbed. From there they were driven down the bank, and along a rocky part of the shore until they were decoyed into a space which was netted in. A dike was built between the Quay and the sea, and the women after catching the sheep and fastening their legs together with "tials", commenced the process of shearing. From our vantage ground we had a view at once novel (at least to me) and picturesque. The women with their bright print dresses girded about them, and shawls wound round their heads, kneeling on the rocks intent on their work, wielded their shears very dextrously, and one by one the sheep were divested of their fleece. Now and then a lamb (the lambs had also been tied to facilitate the numbering of them) would bleat, and the complaining, childlike cry would mingle with the shrill screams of the kittiwakes disturbed from their nests. The sea birds whirling in mid air, showing pure white against the blue of sky and sea were a pretty sight. About three o'clock Mrs. Mitchell and I served lunch to the workers. Sea biscuits with cheese, and huge slices of bread and jam, washed down by milk and porter, were eagerly received by all. Not much time however was spent in eating, soon they were busy again, and by five o'clock the poor, cramped sheep were released, and then they stampeded up the bank, and raced over the isle, not then quite happy until they were joined by their respective offspring. The result of their first rush was the breakage of three cups, a tumbler, and the porter jar. The fleeces were gathered together, and tied into sacks, which were rowed to the Packet. Before leaving for home Mr. and Mrs. Mitchell and I had a walk over the Calf. It is a very pretty isle, clad with the softest of grass, and waving in the breeze was the young bracken. The sail home was accomplished in about the same time, or perhaps rather less, than our outward one. We reached the Manse about seven, and sat down to a ham and egg tea. After having rested a little Mrs. Mitchell and I walked down to Miss Tomison's for the papers, whilst Mr. Mitchell was preparing his Sunday work. Miss Tomison recognised me as the daughter of the Mr. Murray who had been here fifteen years before. We went very early to bed, and after nine hours in the open air, we enjoyed our night's rest exceedingly.

5 Turn of the century sheep-shearing gathering

Sabbath 24th June. Weather still good. It was warm and bright, so I put on my blue blouse. In the forenoon I chose two of the hymns for the service also two for the Sunday School. At twelve we started, and just as we stepped onto the road the bells began. The service was particularly nice and the hymns "Awake my soul, and with the sun", "O'er those gloomy hills of darkness", "Pleasant are thy courts above" were sung heartily. The subject of the discourse was the text from part of the 3rd vr. of the XVIII Ch. of 1st book of Kings (Now Obadiah feared the Lord greatly), and was delivered with much earnestness and vigour. After service as Mrs. Mitchell felt a little sick from the closeness of the church, I undertook to play the hymns "There is a better world they say" and "Shall we gather at the river" for the Sunday school, also I took Mrs. Mitchell's class along with the one I had last Sunday. I was very much taken with them, and they proved quite as polite and tractable as before. 3.30 we partook of dinner, and the afternoon and evening passed very quietly. I wrote to Fitz Roy and Mrs. Barclay, so after the reading and supper we went to post them.

6. Flotta Churchyard

Monday, 25th. A very disagreeable day, foggy and unsettled. A little music, some writing, and reading. I wrote up this diary, finished the "Lilac Sunbonnet", and accompanied Mrs. Mitchell to the church to water the geraniums. Received a letter from Fitz also Tit-Bits. His letter proved very interesting, and was well-written and well put together. The Doctor called in the evening, and talked with Mr. Mitchell for some time. He stayed and had supper then went to visit an old woman who was dying.

Tuesday, 26th. Fair but no sunshine. Mrs. Mitchell, Jacobina and I went shopping, if one could so call it, on the sea. A steamer with groceries, bread, meat, etc. calls every Tuesday if the weather be favourable. One of the men from the steamer rows all those who wish to purchase anything out in a small boat. Several boatfuls were rowed out, and it was very interesting to watch the marketing! Two or three bags of flour were bought, and had to be pulled up on deck on a rope. Each of the purchasers received a handfull of sweeties! Mr. Mitchell paid a visit to old Mrs. Easson who was dying, and I helped to make a light custard for her, in the forenoon. A fisherman brought a dozen crabs to the Manse, they are not much thought of by those who catch then here, lobsters are more valued. After an early tea, I started with Mr. Mitchell for Flotta Calf. He carried his gun and game bag with him, and I took a stick, as the walk before us was a long one. Carlo came with us, and enjoyed it thoroughly, every now and again rolling on his back on the sward. Although the evening was cloudy, the light was shining athwart the Hoy hills, the effect, from the distance, a mist-veiled radiance streaming downwards, was wonderful. Flotta is in form very like a horse shoe, and the bend in the land is filled by the water of Pan Hope. We walked round the swerve in the shore, and reached the hill of Golta, which is covered with heather, and is used by the islanders (who pay for the use of it) for keeping their sheep. It goes by the name of "Commons". Then we reached the part of the shore where Mr. Mitchell moors the small boat he uses for crossing Calf Sound to the Calf. Seven or eight seals appeared within gun-shot, and it was quite amusing to watch how pertly they popped up to gaze at us. Mr. Mitchell thought we might get even a better chance of shooting at them on our return home. Mr. Mitchell rowed over, after the boat had been pulled down, and the gun and game-bag placed in it. Carlo jumped in first, and settled down in the bottom of the boat. We soon crossed the Sound, and jumped ashore near the place where the sheep had been sheared on the Saturday.

After Mr. Mitchell had planted some "Gardener's Garters" which he had brought with him, and I had brought some stones from the shore with which to cover them so as to prevent their being destroyed by the sheep, we walked round the island, which is about half a mile long and less than 1/4 broad. The sheep were scattered over the upper part, and seemed to have quite recovered from the disturbance they had been subjected to. I spent some little time watching two fishermen setting their lobster nets, and I also took some plants of shamrock so that we might plant it in the Manse garden. I found a nest with four downy wee rittacks in it. I had one in my hand for a minute, a pretty little speckled creature. The nests of those Rittacks or Sea-Swallows are scattered over the whole isle, and some even are built on the ware by the shore. About 8 o'clock we started for home, and I rowed across to Golta, where we pulled up the boat, and fastened it securely in its niche in the bank. We made a short detour to see the ruins of what is said to have been an old Episcopal church. It faces Pan Bay, and the "rectory" stands a little higher up. Down on the face of the rocks is a medicinal spring which runs constantly. Mr. Mitchell had a draught from it, but I had scruples about it after seeing the iron floating on the surface. We had not much time to spare, however, as the night was drawing on, and we were getting rather tired. Accordingly we hurried on, and soon came within sight of the Manse. One thing which was rather disappointing was that we did not again see the seals, so the chance of getting one was lost for that day at least. Crab pies for supper, and the clock showing us that we had been four and a half hours at least out of doors, both were good inducements for a hearty meal. I went earlier to bed, and enjoyed the night's rest after my long walk.

Wednesday, 27th. Fair, but cloudy. Received four letters, two from Mamma, one from Maggie and one from Aggie Pullar. I spent some time over my letters, which were all very long and interesting. The afternoon I spent in writing a letter to home, and also in writing up my diary. After tea we all walked to Housca where Mr. Mitchell keeps a small sailing vessel. "Hope" is its name, and it is a trim little boat painted blue and white. Andrew Sutherland helped Mr. Mitchell to launch it, but he could not accompany us, as he was housekeeper, his wife working to the Doctor. However, the wind was favourable, and Mr. Mitchell managed beautifully himself. We sailed through Weddel Sound or the "Rotten Gutter" which lies between Flotta and Fara; although the sky was cloudy, the islands lying round appeared pretty clearly. On our way to the boat in fact we caught a view of Duncansby Head with the sun lighting up the shores of Caithness, also Orphir on the mainland. We passed the buoy which marks the end of Crockness Shoal, and shortly after sailed alongside one of the three coal depots, which lie at anchor in Long Hope. Far in the distance we saw the house of Melsetter in which Mr. Middlemore who owns the estate in Walls, stops. Mr. Mitchell ordered coal to be ready upon his return the following week, and one or two bags were let down the side of the Hulk into our own boat to keep us going until the supply should be conveyed to Flotta. We returned by a different route, passing round by the south side of Flotta. The sky was very changeable, and every now and again the islands around appeared in a different light. With Hackness Point in Walls on our right hand and Innan Neb in Flotta on our left we sailed into Switha Sound. Near Scatwick Bay we saw Spencer's Cave, the front of which is very picturesque, much resembling the doorway into an ancient Gothic Cathedral. With Switha then on our right, and a view of South Ronaldshay, purple in the distance, also Swona and the lovely Pentland Skerries, we passed on the Flotta side (St.) Catherine's Bay, Cave of Banks, then sweeping round we were in Kirk Bay, with the church and Manse overlooking it from the hill. One seal popped up just as we were landing, but we saw no more. We all helped to pull the 'Hope' on shore, and whilst Jacobina took the cargo, namely the bags of coal, up to the Manse, we slowly walked home. We had not used the oars at all, as the breeze carried us along right royally, and altogether the night was a most agreeable one. It was 9.30 before we sat to supper.

Thursday, 28th. Very bright in the morning, but still changeable, ominous clouds surrounding us, and mist hanging o'er the hills of Hoy. We all walked down to Pan to get our letters in the mail bag which the Hoy Head steamer calls for. Very sultry, and depressing. Although the walk is not a long one, we felt rather fatigued. All afternoon spent in "Dolce far niente", then after tea I went to Lurdie a message, accompanied by Carlo, who was rewarded by getting a sea biscuit all to himself. On my return I found Mr. Mitchell prepared for a sail, with his gun and and fishing rod ready. Mrs. Mitchell could not get away, so we started for the shore followed by Carlo. There was no breeze, so we did not use the sails, but I rowed most of the way. It was an ideal night for a sail, not too close, yet bright and warm. We left Kirk Bay about 8 o'clock, and sailed on slowly round by Greeniber Point, where I saw for the first time a great quantity of birds which Mr. Mitchell calls Sea Parrots - Puffins. The name suits them well, as regards their shape. The head and bill very parrot-like, as is the cry they make. Their feathers are mostly black and white, their bills and feet red, the latter being webbed as we could see when they prepared to fly. We had them near us the whole way, either settled in some niche in the rocks, or flying over our heads. On turning Greeniber the scenery becomes magnificent. Switha lying far to the right, in front the long shores of South Ronaldshay whose inhabitants number about two thousand, then on our left Flotta, the rocks on this side are very rugged and precipitous. Although the sea was calm, the rush of the waves, their gradual ebb and flow amongst the caves and rocky recesses sounded in our ears like the distant roll of thunder. Weird even that sound in the serenity of a summer evening, wonderful the scene though the sea but ripples at the base, what must it be to listen there in the violence of a winter storm, or to gaze at it in all its grandeur, whilst the sea leaps high from crag to crag, until the whole is overwhelmed in the rush of the billows, lashed into fury by the gale?

In and out amongst the rocks we paddled on until Stangar Head was turned. We rowed quite close to the mouth of several of the caves, and Mr. Mitchell fired into the darkness to disturb the pigeons if there were any. Several shots however were fired, and the report died away with no success. After we rounded Stangar, nine other boats appeared, the occupants keenly intent on the fishing. Soon we turned again, and from one of the caves we had missed, a flock of pigeons flew out at the first shot. They came so suddenly and unexpectedly that Mr. Mitchell had dropped but one when they had fled from view. Near Greeniber stand two colossal rocks, which have been divided from the land by the continual rush of the sea. They remind one of the Egyptian Sphinx. Several other boats were paddling out and in between the "Cletts" as they are called, and seemed to be successful in their fishing. We followed their example for some time, and caught six "Couths", at least Mr. Mitchell caught five and I caught one. After that we sailed slowly home through Kirk Bay. The ripple on the sea was lovely, as were the reflections cast by an evening sky of tender pink and pearly grey changing as we rowed ashore into a deep orange. Cantick Lighthouse showed white in the distance, and its light reflected on the waters swayed and trembled on every wave. About 11.30 we drew the boat on shore, met there by Mrs. Mitchell and Jacobina who conveyed the but small results of our three and a half hours outing to the Manse. At midnight we sat down to supper, and though the hour was late, we relished our repast, then retired to rest and to a sound sleep.

Friday, 29th. Weather very unsettled. The promises of the evening before, which had been so fair, were not fulfilled. I did not go out all morning, but about one o'clock I had a short walk for about twenty minutes with my book, but as rain came on I had to return. After dinner a young missionary student Mr. Lyons came in. He is at St. Margarets Hope, and had been rowed over by the man he lodges with. We had afternoon tea, and I played once or twice on the violin. About five o'clock, we walked over with him to where his boat was to leave, but as none of his companions were there, and no appearances of the boat starting, he walked back with us and had tea at six o'clock. After tea he left, and we spent the remainder of the evening very quietly; the rain came down in torrents about nine and ten o'clock and continued for some time, but -

Saturday, 30th, dawned gloriously, although the glory died away after breakfast, and the rest of the day until evening was very unsettled. In the forenoon I had a short stroll with my book, but was forced to return on account of a thundery shower. At twelve o'clock Mrs. Easson's funeral took place. The coffin on poles was carried time about by the relatives, the women also sharing the burden for a time. The procession followed the coffin bearers to the churchyard, where the service was held. We all felt very unsettled, like the weather, and excepting a walk to the church before tea, the day passed very quietly indeed. A magnificent sunset crowned the day which had dawned so magnificently. The Manse is very pleasantly situated, in the midst of green fields and rising crops. It stands high up, and has a commanding view, of the surrounding district. It fronts to the south, and overlooks Kirk Bay; at the left side, also on the shore, is the church and the graveyard. The Manse garden lies to the north, and is very fertile. One hardy plant that seems to flourish in this far northern climate is "London Pride", but poppies, lilies and pansies are not far behind. One thing that strikes me very much, is the song of the lark, which one hears at all hours. Lightly, joyously they trill their melodies at "Heaven's Gate" at dawn, in the heat of noon-day, and in the calm of a summer twilight.

7. Flotta Church, embroidered organ cloth

Sunday, July 1st. A bright morning, but later on the rain came, and the day continued showery. The service passed off nicely, the sermon being from the text Romans XIII vs. XIV "But put ye on the Lord Jesus Christ". I again took a class, the same one that I had before. A good many were absent both in church and Sunday school. After dinner we settled down for the afternoon; I read from "Life and Work". After tea I wrote home, and then spent an hour or two playing on the organ, finishing off with the hymn "The day thou gavest, Lord is ended".

Before walking to the Pillar with our letters, we had the Reading and partook of supper. We enjoyed the turn in the open after the rain very much. The air was very cool and pleasant, and the bluey-grey of the sky with its dash of saffron, was reflected very clearly and beautifully on the surface of Pan Hope. About 11.30 we went to bed.

Monday, 2nd. A glorious day. I walked to Lurdie to buy a stone for sharpening the scythe, as Mr. Mitchell wanted to begin the hay cutting. I met several of the islanders, and they were all very agreeable. They seldom pass without a "Good Morning" to you. On my return I had a little music until dinner-time. In the afternoon, we all went out to the hay field, where Mr. Mitchell started to work again, whilst Mrs. Mitchell sewed and I read. About five o'clock Jacobina brought us tea on a tray and it was very pleasant having it in the hay-field, in the midst of the newly-cut sweet scented hay. I then took a lesson from Jacobina in singling turnips, and rather enjoyed what was quite a new experience for me. At six we all went up to visit Mrs. Robertson, Jacobina's Mother, who has been an invalid for fifteen years. She suffers from dreadful pain in her head and limbs, and Mr. Mitchell read a chapter from Romans, and said a prayer. She was very anxious for us to stay longer, but as Mr. Wyllie was expected at seven, we had to leave, as it was he was awaiting us when we got back. We then had tea, and after the gentlemen had enjoyed a smoke, I played several pieces on the violin. What with music and talking the night soon passed, and it was one o'clock before Mr. Wyllie left, and we went to bed. We had planned an excursion for Tuesday night.

Tuesday, 3rd. I awoke about eight o'clock and the rain was coming down in torrents. It had been pretty heavy during the night, but after breakfast it cleared and gradually the sun appeared through the clouds, so that by afternoon they were dispersed. I wrote a letter to Fitz-Roy, and Mr. Mitchell and I walked to the Post with it, so that it might reach him by Thursday, his birthday. The steamer was late, so we did not await its arrival. At Lurdy we stopped to procure some necessaries for our fishing excursion at night. Then on our way home we called on Mrs. Simpson, whose husband died a fortnight ago. She was very pleased to see Mr. Mitchell, as she feels lonely now. However she was looking forward she said to the return of her son Sutherland, who is an assistant professor in Edinburgh University. On reaching the school, we went in to see Mr. Wyllie, and to let him know, that we intended to carry out our plan, if the weather continued favourable. He took us in to see the school and scholars. Miss Thomson was busy in one room whilst Mr. Wyllie's own class was in the other. One boy called Donald Thomson, in Miss Thomson's class recited "Somebody's Mother" very clearly and nicely. Then Mr. Wyllie made one of his boys sing "The Little Fisher Boy". He had a good, strong voice. I was also shown some of the drawing-books. One belonging to a boy Work, showed great promise. The drawings were able and neat. As it was past two o'clock we hurried home to dinner. About four o'clock, I went out to the field, and did a little turnip singling again. I am getting a little better at it but still slow. After tea we rested and read until Mr. Wyllie came at eight. Mrs. Mitchell did not accompany us, as she did not feel well enough, and it was late (nine) before we set out. We had two rods and a draw-line with us. Mr. Mitchell and I took turn about with the rowing, and as the sea was fairly calm, we got on nicely. The wind was rather high for going to Switha as we had intended, so we just paddled about near Greeniber Pt. I caught two fish, one a "Couth", the other a "Lythe". Altogether we had twenty-two, and had it not been for the "Sea-monsters" we saw, probably our haul would have been bigger. It was just as we rounded Greeniber, going out, that we first saw the whale. Mr. Wyllie was convinced that it was a porpoise, but considering its size we took it to be a small whale. However, we rowed quickly to the side, and Mr. Mitchell jumped out onto a shelving rock, and held the boat close in to the side. After a while we rowed out again, and continued our fishing, keeping pretty much in to the side. Numberless times did the monster rise leading us to believe by the distances between each rise, and the time that elapsed, that there were several of them. New experiences are plentiful with me in the meantime, and it was most interesting, entertaining, and exciting to watch the upheavals at unexpected places, generally behind our boat, of the "Leviathan of the Deep". Once it rose behind us just about two rod lengths away. Mr. Mitchell says he is sure it must have been forty feet at any rate in length. It would have been very alarming had the monster ventured much nearer our boat! We rowed ashore about midnight, but it was quite clear, and on reaching home, we saw to take supper by the night light. By one o'clock I was in bed, and I slept very soundly, after having spent almost the whole day in the open air, either on land or sea. We had divided the spoil equally with Mr. Wyllie, who seemed to have enjoyed the expedition immensely.

8. The Mitchell family

Wednesday, 4th. Weather beautiful. Spent a quiet forenoon; writing up into my diary everything worthy of note, and then spent some time at the piano. After dinner, about four o'clock, Mr. Mitchell took me to see the "Gloups" at Stangar Head. It is a fairly long walk, but going, we paid a visit to a family of the name Simpson. About a quarter of an hour afterwards, we again set forth. It was breezy, but the sun was shining brightly, and as we had taken the glass with us, we got a splendid view of the country, sea and islands around us. The Gloups are two tremendous holes in the earth, very deep and rocky down a bit, and the sea rushing and roaring below. The land here by the sea is very rocky and rugged, but it appeals to one very strongly after the quiet pasture land. Mr. Mitchell took me to a part below "Dass", which is as far as he knows the only place on the island where the ocean is not seen, and yet take but a step or two, and there it is, blue in the distance. With the glass I had a good view of Kirkwall, Stromness, St. Mary's, South Ronaldsay, Switha, Cantick Lighthouse, the coal depots, Hoy and its hills, and a vast surface of the sea, with here and there a small boat, or a steamer. A mere speck on the horizon both with glass and the naked eye was what we took for a yacht. Later on (after tea) we saw it pass between Flotta and Switha, and it proved to be a schooner. After we had seen all we went to see, we turned homewards, and reached the Manse just in time for tea. We had thought of going on another fishing excursion, but the night was cloudy and the wind was too high, so we did not go. The evening passed very quietly.

Thursday, the 5th. Proved very disagreeable. In the early morning it had rained very heavily, and at eight o'clock although fair, and the clouds breaking, still the wind was very high. After breakfast Mr. Mitchell hurried away to catch the steamer, so that he might post two letters, and send a telegram to Brechin, to let them know that I could not get away, owing to the weather. I donned my waterproof and went to meet him, but the roads especially where grassy were very wet indeed. Shortly after we came home the post came in and I received a letter from mamma. I was glad to get it and to know that they had gone to Stonehaven. In the forenoon I made good progress with my knitting, and was very industrious until dinner-time. After dinner I read until four o'clock, when we prepared to pay a few visits. Accordingly about five o'clock Mr. and Mrs. Mitchell and I set out for Everhowe, to see a poor old woman who is very ill. She could understand all that was said to her, but yes and no were the only words we could make out in her speech. Mr. Mitchell read and prayed, and soon after we took our leave. Next door live the poor old couple of eighty years of age. So as we were so near, we went to see them again. The old woman was looking a little better, and was sitting before her peat fire baking bannocks. Her husband was in bed, but the place was so small, I could not get in far enough to see him. Mrs. Mitchell had not been there before and I think she was as glad as we were to get into the fresh air once more. At another house where the grandfather was bad with cold, Mr. Mitchell again engaged in prayer, and read a chapter. About 6.30 we reached the Manse again, and I enjoyed my tea very much, as the long walk in the fair breeze had given me an appetite. About eight o'clock we all went to pay a visit at "Bay View", the residence of Mrs. Haye. However she was not at home, so we did not stay very long. Arthur, Violet, Mabel and Charles Albert all helped to entertain us! They were very shy, so we had to do most of the talking. We walked slowly home again, and as Mrs. Mitchell was very tired did not go out that night.

Friday, 6th. Still very stormy, we did not go out all forenoon, but we had a visit from Willie Hett, who is home on furlough. He was wounded at Paardeberg, in the arm, and thirteen bits of bone were taken out. From Paardeberg the wounded were conveyed in waggons to Wynberg. At Wynberg Lady Roberts spoke to him, and her husband had also wished each of them "Good Luck". Hett was Orderly to Captain Rennie of the Black Watch. On board coming home there were 620 wounded soldiers, with only one Doctor and one sister to attend to them. The Doctor, who drank, died but four and a half days before the vessel reached Southampton. The field hospitals contained all who suffered from Enteric or Typhoid fevers, and in fact all the cases infectious or otherwise were lying together. Down in Cape Town Hospitals the Boer and Briton invalids were together, and Hett says the Boers were better treated than our own men. Captain Rennie went to carry General Wanchope to camp, after he had been shot. Lord Methuen had given orders that firing should be stopped until the wounded had all been carried into safety. However, before the proper time had expired, Methuen had changed the order, and Rennie had not got far from the Boer trenches when firing was resumed. However, he escaped unhurt, although a shell had burst just behind him. General Wanchope was well beloved by the Highland Brigade, and Hett said that he had to carry out Methuen's orders in spite of the fact that he thought it wrong, and knew of a better plan himself. Someone of the soldiers had been asking Methuen for more officers, and although he had a number around him doing nothing he said "Take one of the Infantry Officers". Now there were but two of them, and one was wounded whilst the other was not much use. Methuen then said to Rennie "Have you no men, you can send?" "No, Sir, I take my orders from my General" (Wanchope). Hett whilst attending to his Master and the other officers had a splendid opportunity for hearing many interesting things, but he says he heard many which he may not tell, but which will come out in time. Methuen is not well-liked, and from what Hett says is not a good soldier. He heard "Pole-Carew" say that he would not obey an order of Methuen's, except he thought it right. The air of South Africa seemed to have suited him (Hett); and he said that the heat was not so great as to affect him, although when he washed his shirt, it was dry in the sun by the time he had bathed.

The water of Modder River he did not object to, but then as he was with the officers, the water was filtered. The forced march to Coodesberg took two days, and the object of it viz. to intercept two Boer Commandos was attained. The first day they accomplished eight miles, the second twenty-two. Several of the men had thought it hard, but Hett did not consider it so. General Wanchope, who was said to have been riddled with bullets, had as far as Hett knew only three wounds, but the mistake had been made owing to the fact that the General's nephew was very badly wounded (riddled). This young orderly left for the seat of war in October and returned to this country on the lst of May. His wound was a very serious one, and although his arm is a good deal better, still the muscle power is out of it altogether. He will probably be pensioned, but may still continue to be Captain Rennie's orderly. He stayed two and a half hours with us, so we had a good talk about the war, he is getting one shilling and eleven pence in the meantime, a day. Shortly after he had gone we had dinner, and then Mr. Mitchell and I sallied forth to pay a few more visits. We went first to see the Norquays of Quayness with whom Mamma and Papa lodged on their visit to Orkney. The old woman was not well, she has a growth on her breast bone which is affecting her health, the young couple were looking healthy, and James showed me a very light coloured seal-skin, which he had cured. On leaving them we went to another Mrs. Norquay - and found her very ill indeed. She had not spoken one word that day, that they could make out. However, after Mr. Mitchell had read and prayed, she said several things in answer to his questions, very distinctly. Mr. Mitchell promised to go again the next day, and with that we left. On our way down the hill we went in for a few minutes to see an old man, by name Dan Sandieson. He was sitting at a corner of his table looking very comfortable and happy, and enjoying an egg to his tea. He had no cloth, but the table looked clean, and he had everything at hand; the salt in its cellar, sugar basin, a plate of brannocks, and his cup of tea and egg. The peat fire was burning in the middle of the room, still the room was not smoky, the smoke indeed seemed to make its way out at the square chimney above, very well. It looked very cheery, and by the side was standing a little three-legged pot, in which I presumed the old man had boiled his egg. A big black kettle and a brown tea pot were also on the hearth, and nearby stood the bucket of peats with which he replenished the fire. Considering that Dan is a bachelor, his house looked very clean and cosy, as for himself, he was a picture of content, smacking his lips after each spoonful of egg. He would have made a good study for an artist, for he is a fine looking old man, with a ruddy complexion, and pure white hair and beard. He was looking forward to killing and eating a three year old cock, and it was amusing to hear him answer Mr. Mitchell as to how he would set about the picking and cooking of it. Knowing that it was drawing near our tea-time, we soon left the old gentleman to complete his repast in peace. After tea I read a good deal, and wrote two letters, one to Brechin and the other to Stonehaven. About nine o'clock we started for the School house, where stamps are got. Mr. Wyllie was having a stroll in his neatly kept garden, and after having a look around it, we accepted his invitation to come in, and "rest our shanks", as he expressed it. His housekeeper Miss Stuart treated Mr. Mitchell and Mr. Wyllie to a glass of whisky, but Mrs. Mitchell and I who of course did not care to take spirits, enjoyed a biscuit, while the gentlemen sipped away. Mr. Wyllie has a very nice room, well furnished, and with plenty of books, and we stayed cracking to him until almost twelve o'clock. On our return to the Manse, we took supper, and went almost immediately after to bed. A lot had been said, heard and done, during the day, and we rested well.

Saturday 7th. Wind still high, but the sun bright. I accompanied Mr. Mitchell to Windbreak, where he arranged with Dan Sutherland for our going into Kirkwall on Monday. Except a walk to the church in the afternoon to water the flowers, we were not out again; but spent the day very quietly indeed.

9. Stromness doorway

Sunday 8th. I awoke about four o'clock, and my room was flooded with sunshine and I fell asleep again with the thought that we were to have a lovely Sabbath, but no, after we had started for Housca, the sky became overcast, and by the time we reached the shore it had begun to drizzle. Mr. Brown who was rowed over by one of his parishioners just landed at the pier as we walked on to it. After Mr. Mitchell had arranged to have the sacrament at Fara on the 1st Sunday in August, we got aboard, and the sails being set, we went over nicely. After landing on the shore of Fara, we had not far to walk to the church. It is a mission church, and is a very nice compact little building, which is seated to hold about 120. Mrs. Mitchell and I went into the vestry where I took off my waterproof, and then we took our seats at the back of the church. Bye and bye the congregation dropped in, and about 12.15 the service began. There is no pulpit, but a sort of reading-desk which serves both as pulpit and lectern. Of course there is no organ or harmonium, and Mr. Mitchell has to be both preacher and precentor. Four psalms were sung, two chapters read, and after that and the usual prayers, Mr. Mitchell delivered a very good sermon from the text "And (take) the sword of the Spirit, which is the word of God" St. Paul's epistle to the Ephesians 6th Ch. part of the 17th vs. There were about twenty-five of the congregation present, but the weather would probably be the excuse for the absent ones! After the collection was taken, and the benediction given, the people dispersed. I was introduced to Mrs. Brown and her daughter, they seem very nice indeed. Then we left the vestry, and set sail again for Flotta. Dinner awaited us on our return, and we were not long in before Mr. Brown appeared, besides taking the service, he also had the Sabbath school. Mr. Brown is the Fara missionary or preacher, and I was rather taken with him. He is very patriarchal in appearance, beautiful white hair and beard, with good brown eyes, with a fire flashing from them whenever anyone differs from him in opinion. He impressed me as being a man of great determination, very dogmatic, brooking no interference, passionate, and yet with an appearance of wisdom, and a knowledge of the world. Jacobina brought in a tray with afternoon tea, and about 5.40 Mr. Brown left, Mr. Mitchell accompanying him part of the way, as he had to call on the family who were mourning the loss of the mother (Norquay).

Monday, 9th. Raining in torrents, after packing up, we waited for the post, which did not come, until nearly two o'clock. Then we had dinner, and after all our necessary preparations were made we walked to the pier in Pan Hope. Dan the boatman had not appeared so Mr. Mitchell dispatched Tom Hett to fetch him, and we waited in a boat shed. Jacobina had come also to carry my bag, and after Dan and Willie came, we were rowed to the Packet, "The Happy Return". After the sails were set, the men spread a tarpaulin over part of the deck, then Mrs. Mitchell and I got in below. Dan brought out the compass, and Mr. Mitchell steered, once Mrs. Mitchell tried her hand at it. The rain came down steadily, and every now and then we were becalmed. We ought to have reached Kirkwall in two hours after leaving, had we had a fair wind, but with sometimes no wind, and when it came, very light, we took five hours. At nine o'clock we reached Scapa Pier, and then we had a walk of about one mile and a half to Kirkwall. The road, although a good one, was of course in bad condition, very muddy, however we were glad to be on "Terra Firma" once more, so we walked on quite briskly. The land near Kirkwall on the one side was cultivated, but on the left not so, or at least it had been at one time, but had been allowed to waste again. Beautiful stretches of meadow, bright with buttercups, and lovely grasses with the rain-drops clinging to them, clumps of the wild Iris, with a flower just out here and there. Glad were we to reach the town and make for the Royal Hotel, where after refreshing ourselves, we sat down to a ham and egg tea, or supper? The rain was not over, in fact it poured all night. I went to bed soon after supper, as I was tired out, but, whether from excitement or over-fatigue, sleep refused to visit my eye-lids.

At 7.30 we were called, we had meant to get up at 6, but as a telegram had come the night before, stating that the steamer would not arrive from Lerwick until 9.30, we stayed some time longer in bed! After breakfast, it was still raining, we started for the pier, but judge of our annoyance, when we found that owing to the fog, the steamer would not be in until about mid-day. There was nothing for it, but to return to the town, and perhaps it was just as well, as it gave me an opportunity of seeing it. We went in to the Cathedral, and saw through it. It is supposed to have been built about the 11th or 12th century, and it has all the appearances of antiquity. The carving at the doorway is all worn with age. It has a splendid clock, with gold figures on a black face. The front part is like a large reception room, with huge columns supporting it on either side, and a great deal of carving, but no seats. Several stained glass windows, memorial ones, and two or three magnificent crypts. One, to the memory of John Rae, Arctic explorer, was very good. His figure was carved out of marble, and represented lying with his gun by his side, and one arm doubled under his head; it is a most magnificent piece of sculpture. This part is not used for worship, as the congregation is not large enough. A large door, with glass upper ornamented, encloses a portion for the worship. It has a very ancient look, and the close, musty smell emphasises the fact that it is old. The boy took us up a steep winding stairway to the bell-tower, where he tolled three bells, one after another. On reaching the top, we got out onto the parapet, although I walked right round, it was too wet and misty to see anything. However, just on the left I saw the ruins of the Bishop's Palaces, but had the weather been favourable, the view would have been extensive. The old keeper said an entrance fee of 6d each by order of the council was required. We did not believe him, but gave up the money rather than make a fuss. His manoeuvres to get a tip over and above from us were most amusing, but he did not manage to circumvent us! After we had seen all the Cathedral we returned to the hotel, and sat there for a short time, then walked once more to the pier. By this time the clouds were breaking, and the rain had stopped. We had a long wait for the steamer, but once it came in sight, we were very much interested in watching its progress into Kirkwall Bay; and when it was alongside the pier, we had plenty to occupy our time. The Captain (Taylor) commanding from his bridge, the bustle and excitement of people coming off, and of others taking their places, and securing berths, all was new to me. Mr. and Mrs. Mitchell came on board with me, and spoke to the stewardess, then we watched the sheep, pigs and cattle being driven down the gangway. They went down very quietly, all except the pigs, and they made a great disturbance, squealing frightfully. Sawdust was scattered at the foot of the gangway, but notwithstanding one of the cows slipped and fell on its side. After all the cargo was boarded, and the passengers had said goodbye to friends ashore, the steamer started. I waved to my friends as long as I could see them, and then I went down to the ladies' cabin, where I sat until three o'clock, when I had dinner with a Miss Ward (who knew Mrs. Perie's sister in Kirkwall). We had roast beef and new potatoes, and tapioca pudding flavoured with bitter almonds. I enjoyed it very much indeed. Then I went up and sat on deck with Miss Ward and a Mrs. Irvine, a captain's widow. The sky had gradually cleared until the whole was blue, with white and pale heliotrope clouds on the horizon. The sun was shining gloriously, and the sea was deep blue, and very calm, we steamed along beautifully. I sat writing, and gazing around, all afternoon. We saw a full-rigged vessel, painted a delicate crimson, and the sun glancing on it, showed it up, and varied the colour. Soon we passed it, and then the sails seemed to get darker and darker, as the sunlight slanted off it, until the whole seemed in shape and colour like a beacon. The herring boats were scattered on the ocean on all sides. It was a lovely scene. At seven we had tea and toast in the saloon and it was refreshing. Back on deck once more, and had great fun watching the gentlemen play various games. In one, a thread and needle race, several of we ladies joined, and spent a fine time. Later on we had an impromptu concert, and I sang "Annie Laurie", whilst a lady artist accompanied me on the piano. The music saloon was soon well filled, and the gentlemen gave a variety of songs, while I played accompaniments. I did not go to bed, as the steamer was to reach the city at 2.30 a.m. Along with Mrs. Irvine and Miss Fair, I stayed on deck all the time, for indeed it would have been a pity to miss the passage (on deck) on such a glorious night. The sun had but just set, falling as it were into the ocean, and throwing towards us a parting gift of radiating light; and the moon rose slowly, getting purer and clearer in the rising, whilst we sped over the waters at the rate of, say, 16 miles an hour. The "City of Aberdeen" is a splendid steamer, and beautifully fitted up. At Peterhead, a tug came off to take the fisher girls ashore. They had been singing some boat songs, and before leaving they sang several of Moodie and Sankie's hymns. One "God be with you, till we meet again" sounded, from our position above, very prettily. When the tug came up, they had to be lifted on, as it plunged and heaved so, that there was as often as not a good space between our steamer and it. One hundred and eighty of the girls were carried over, and then the tug steamed off, whilst we made way once more. We all started singing "Auld Lang Syne", but soon the voices died away, as each vessel headed for different parts. At 2.30 we reached Aberdeen, and the two ladies, and a gentleman home from India saw me ashore, where I secured a light porter, and started for Union Street. I reached there at about a quarter to three, and found that my cousin had been at the pier at 2 o'clock, but of course did not find the steamer there. I demolished several tongue sandwiches, with a glass of milk, and hastened into bed. I slept soundly till 8.30, when my cousin came in with a letter from Mamma, saing they could not be in Aberdeen that day, so I left the city with the 10 train for Stonehaven. Another fine day, very warm, rather thundery. At Stonehaven station, Mamma and Aunt Alice, Fitz-Roy and Herbert were awaiting me, and we drove out to New Mains. Dada arrived from Brechin at 1.30, and my tongue went constantly for about three hours! In the afternoon Aunt Alice drove in for Mrs. Hampton, whilst Mr. Hampton, and Mr. and Mrs. Campbell and the baby walked out. We spent a very pleasant afternoon and evening, walking about, inspecting the farm, and otherwise enjoying ourselves. About 8 o'clock our friends left, and, we escorted them a little bit.

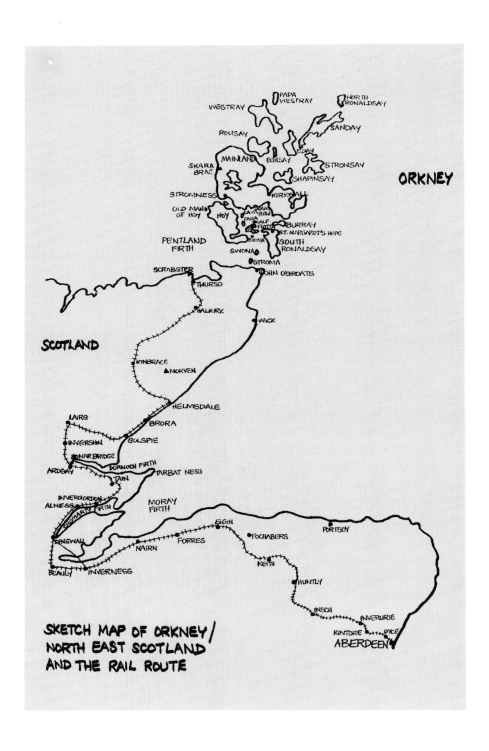

SKETCH MAP OF ORKNEY/
NORTH EAST SCOTLAND
AND THE RAIL ROUTE

36

Flotta Church on the shore of Kirk Bay

CHRONICLE II

The Journey 1989

Sitting up in bed, we both enjoyed a glass of Baileys "Original Irish Cream" and reflected on the adventures to come. We had travelled to Aberdeen in order to begin at the same point as our predecessor.

After a nine hour train journey we were thankful to reach the Western Guest House and to relax. The function of the Bed and Breakfast is so much more than bed and breakfast. Its importance to our trip cannot be overestimated - somewhere to wash away the rigours of the day in preparation for the next, a place to enjoy a measure of domesticity, a haven in which to stop seeing and experiencing so that we can report on what we have already seen. Each evening having written our diaries we planned to exchange them to read the other's recollections, and finally to combine them into a 1989 diary to accompany Brenda Murray's.

Our day of departure from Aberdeen began quite differently from hers. A battery-operated alarm clock woke us at 7.30 a.m., we breakfasted at 9 o'clock, three hours after Miss Murray had boarded the train. In our defence we should say we could not have had breakfast before 8.30 anyway in our guest house. And she had bedded down at 10.30 and slept, whereas we had talked until 3 a.m. Our train did not leave until 1.05 so we had a few hours in which to see something of Aberdeen.

The "Granite City" was serene on a quiet, still summer morning, the grey sky in perfect harmony with the buildings. The air was cool, not cold, clear and, though not sunny, bright. Good photographic light. We walked the full length of Union Street, largely made up of modern shops and 1960s concrete facades. We had anticipated more grand, old granite buildings, but apart from the Sheriff's Court, some churches, and a Salvation Army Citadel complete with Transylvanian Gothic towers, they eluded us. At the harbour we photographed a red and yellow cargo ship, a wonderfully colourful spectacle against the grey of the city. Passing Provost Ross' House, the oldest in Aberdeen, we visited Marischal College, a very ornate University College built in 1903.

In the centre of the city, the churchyard of the Kirk of St. Nicholas was an eerie, enclosed haven away from the commercial street. A huge granite gateway with a 20 feet high row of classical columns on either side leads the wanderer through the dark shade of sycamore trees passing densely-packed graves large and grand, mostly blackened or mossy with age. Many are "table" gravestones, with just a gap and bare earth underneath a huge slab some three feet off the ground, and neither of us had seen these before. The graveyard is almost like a room with the sycamores providing a bright green canopy. A rose garden with seats and fountain and lots of pigeons completes the churchyard which became the heart of our Aberdeen.

After collecting our luggage and making friends with "Lucky the Left-Luggage Cat", we boarded the train and settled into the carriage. The journey we were embarking on was, apart from Flotta itself, the most important part of the trip. Miss Murray described what she saw in such minute detail, and we would follow all her description of the landscapes, even if we could not imitate every aspect of her own journey. We were well-prepared, with Bartholomew's 4 miles-to-the-inch map of north-east Scotland spread out on the table, along with our copies of the 1900 diary, our notebooks, cameras, sandwiches, orange juice....Two cans of Muscadet clicked together, and we toasted our adventure.

Looking around the "Sprinter" train, there were many things to astonish a Miss Murray of 1900: the purr of the train's diesel engine, the automatic sliding doors, the tannoy announcement of imminent arrival at stations. Should we have stopped at nothing today and travelled in period costume? No, we were wearing trousers. And, we were in a non-smoking carriage, very important to us. Presumably Miss Murray would have minded less if her fellow travellers indulged, as it was then considered an aid to health.

This three-carriage local train went at great speed, making photography through its grimy windows a gamble. In Miss Murray's day photography was only for the wealthy. Conceivably she could have borrowed a camera for her trip but it would have been noteworthy if so, and she made no mention. The catering arrangements she enjoyed in 1900 are too much to expect from dispute-ridden British Rail in 1989. We purchased our pre-packed, plastic-wrapped refreshments from a trolley plying in the aisles. We recalled her menu with nostalgia: "*At Bonar Bridge Station we partook of delightful plates of pea soup, also tongue sandwiches with fine keen mustard.*"

Leaving Aberdeen, we saw the beige-shaded areas on our map turn into beige estates of new homes, sports centres and warehouses, no 'open country to Oyne' so far. But, then the countryside opened up. Meadows and cornfields, hay rolls, woods, the meandering River Urie, the rugged and forbidding black

41

outline of Millstone Hill, all came into view in bright yellow sunlight under a cloudless blue sky. At Insch, the signalman was wearing the kilt. The inscription on the station building is 1880. Miss Murray would have looked at that, and we began to feel close to her. We passed a pig farm, not smart prize winners but fluid-fleshed belly-porkers basking in the sun.

The sunlit landscape through which we travelled was beautiful and rolling. There were isolated stone farms, lush grass, ranks of conifers up the hillsides, heather bright in the sun on the hilltops, vast elderflower bushes with fat clumps of heavy flowerheads, wild dog rose, cow parsley, and rosebay willowherb.

Increasingly we believed that Miss Murray must have had a guide book at her side. At Huntly, we tried to see her 'many fine buildings...on the outskirts of the town'. Her mention of 'Portsoy' was another indication as the line goes through Keith and not up to the coast at this point. And looking out from the station at Elgin we could only imagine that it was a guide book that led her to write 'a very fashionable place with a great many large houses.'

Approaching Nairn we skirted the Moray Firth and saw on the far side a long line of cliffs, above deep blue water and topped by rolling green velvet. Travelling along the water's edge we had our first sight of the road bridge between the Firths of Moray and Beauly, leading from Inverness, across to the Black Isle and beyond. The train ride was broken in Inverness. The railway line crosses the River Ness, flowing from the Loch, via a bridge which was washed away in a storm in February, 1989, not six months before our visit. British Rail had laid on a bus to Dingwall where we rejoined the train. In terms of adherence to the diary this detour was unfortunate, but nevertheless we tried to turn it to our advantage, and it worked.

We asked a taxi driver if, in the half-hour available before the bus departed, we could be driven to the shore to see the Firth. The driver, friendly and understanding, suggested he could take us to

Kessock ferry for four pounds and fifty pence or to the northern edge of Loch Ness for seven pounds. We took the first option and were rewarded by a bonus en route. He took us to see the remaining two stone arches of the washed-away railway bridge, stopping on the adjacent road bridge for us to leap out and take photographs. Asked if he charged extra for guided tours and commentary he replied "Ach, it's just nice to show people your town."

The Kessock Ferry, now redundant, was the only way to the Black Isle peninsula other than a 12-mile drive, until nine years ago when the new road bridge was built. The views in all directions from Kessock are superb. We looked back at Inverness and the driver bemoaned a hillside of new houses. Trees had been felled to make room for them and there was much local controversy. A little fringe of trees remains along the skyline but only local outcry prevented these being cleared as well.

We also looked up the Beauly Firth, across to the Black Isle (so-named for its very fertile black soil) and past the new bridge down the Moray Firth. In the distance was the rounded, slightly hazy shape of Ben Wyvis. Driving us back, our guide pointed out the new harbour opened by the Queen two years before, logs piled up on the quay, oil supply ships. Inverness, he said, was being used because of dock disputes at Aberdeen. A vivid picture of the waterfront scene lingers with us.

Back at the station we discovered the bus had already filled and departed early. Another would be along shortly. An open-backed van full of luggage was pointed out and the driver told us to add ours to the pile. Readily we complied, then panicked, looking for his British Rail uniform. Seeing none, we wondered if we would see our bags again? No confidence was inspired when he closed the back revealing the name: Van Rental by Sharps Reliable Wrecks.

Marvellous aerial views of Inverness and the Beauly Firth were visible from the coach when high up on the new bridge. We looked down onto the little promontory of South Kessock where we had been with our taxi driver. The shimmering waters were blue, alive with little yachts. On the Black Isle, a road sign said 'Dingwall 12, John o'Groats 126'. We felt strange travelling by road, missing the train already, and were glad that Dingwall was not far.

In the smart but modest town of Dingwall we boarded a train and sat down with some urgency, fetching map, camera, paper and pen onto the table. At 4.50 p.m., our scheduled departure time, the driver switched the engine off. Miss Murray's train stopped 'a little' here. Ours stopped altogether. At 5.20 p.m. the journey was again underway. After some miles we saw three oil platforms in the distance on the approach to Invergordon. When we could remember to look back, the reward was a beautiful view of sparkling sea and misty hills. We travelled along the shore of Dornoch Firth, with the mountains of Easter Ross rising in front of us. Along the upper banks of the Firth, hillsides thickly clad with firs sloped steeply down into the water, which reflected the clear blue sky above.

At 6.30, we were waiting at Lairg Station and feeling tired, having scribed and photographed intensely since 7.30 a.m. Unwrapping our sandwiches, we remained nevertheless on full guard, ready to grab our cameras if necessary. The scenery along the whole journey presented thousands of 'photo-opportunities'. It was a shame therefore that we had to compose so quickly, before the 'view' disappeared behind a bank of trees. We found the best idea was to have the cameras permanently clapped to our faces, like a duel - guns at....well, teatime, rather than dawn.

The line turns a right angle at the end of Loch Shin, and we headed east along Strath Fleet. Meandering between heather-topped mountains and rocky outcrops, there are long stretches with no habitation, then an isolated croft, or a cluster, with fields of sheep nearby. We turned toward the coast and could see far across the mouth of the blue Dornoch Firth to Whiteness Sands. Further along we looked to Tarbat Ness, and then the land slipped away and our view was of open sea. To the left were magnificent mountains, whilst on the seaward side, sandy bays with not a soul to be seen. Miss Murray had described this exactly as we saw it; on Lothbeg Point we saw a flock of a dozen or so cormorants on a rock at the water's edge.

The station at Helmsdale is pretty. Navy blue and cream is the standard colour scheme for buildings on Scotrail stations, no matter their shape, size or function. Pulling away from Helmsdale station with its pink flowers in hanging baskets, we had a view of the town on the hillside and the River Helmsdale leading to the sea. As we coursed through Kildonan Strath and on to Loch an Ruathair, the setting sun was reflected in the water. The whole scene was near monochrome, silvery shimmers and silhouettes.

Snow barriers line the track intermittently on both sides, preventing the winter drifts blocking the line. On the edge of Forsinard Station, we read a notice: 'Stop, obtain token before proceeding'. There is a single track at this point, and a single token, so that only one driver at a time can enter the stretch. In the fields were row after row of tufty plants with white, fluffy flowers. Was this the 'cotton' to which Miss Murray refers after passing Nairn? We caught sight of a fairytale castle in the distance, and we were told from the aisle that this was Lochdu Lodge. The mountain behind it in the far distance was Morven.

We noticed the temperature dropping, and were surprised how quickly evening fell. The sun was gone, clouds had gathered and we both shivered. After a short stop at Georgemas Junction, where we noticed that the station house was up for lease, the train split, the other two carriages going on to Wick.

In the sun again at Thurso Station, we were welcomed by the sight of a wheelbarrow full of flowers in a spacious, airy waiting room. A taxi took us to our guest house at the top of the town with a view of the Pentland Firth. Though tired after the seven hour train ride, a short walk down through the quiet, immaculate streets refreshed us. The houses were small-scale, single-storey, with colourful flower beds. Stepping through a passage between the terraces suddenly brought us onto the 'front'. Such a view: the wide, sandy beach and various headlands, and islands creeping across the horizon. We sat on the sea wall dangling our legs.

Here began an unforgettable hour. The sun setting behind Scrabster, the cliffs a solid black outline, the brilliant sky, and the yellow gleam on the flat sea. To the east was an entirely different range of colour, daylight shades in contrast to approaching night. The red stone cliffs of Dunnet Head, pink-blue sky reflected in pink-blue water. Black-headed gulls flew around us, and waders patrolled the shore. The only sounds were the wash of the sea and the gulls' cries. We were conscious that the line of the beach is the top of Scotland, the top of Britain.

Returning to our room, we watched the Wimbledon tennis finals on the portable television provided, realising that this is a luxury of the modern age. Counting up our rolls of film, we found that we had taken almost 300 photographs already.

As we took the taxi to the ferry at Scrabster in the morning, we thought how Miss Murray 'procured a trap' for the same journey in 1900. We were also aware that she completed the entire trip from Aberdeen via Thurso to Flotta in one day, something which, despite the wonders of modern transport, timetables no longer permit.

The P & O office was busy, but we managed to secure seats on deck at the stern of the St. Ola, thinking that sea sickness would be best avoided here. Not so! We did not account for the treacherous waters of the Pentland Firth, whose strong currents, along with the ship's stabilisers, result in a very uncomfortable crossing, even in calm weather. Though torrential rain awoke us, it was now dry and warm, though overcast. Heavy scudding clouds raced across the sky. It was misty out at sea, and the big question of the morning was whether or not we would see the Old Man of Hoy?

The cliffs of Hoy appeared ever closer on our right, bright red sandstone with green grassy tops. Sections of cliff were invisible, completely shrouded in mist, then a stretch cleared and came into view. But, the low cloud remained hanging as if suspended at the cliff-tops. The alcoves in the cliffs, between each protruding few yards of rock were mist-filled too. Inevitably, our views were partly obscured but the effect was eerie and primeval. The Old Man emerged from the mists, and half the boat swarmed to look and photograph. The Old Man looked completely different in shape, height and scale from each direction as we sailed past, and then disappeared into the mist again, to reappear in the distance before we lost sight of it completely. Sea-birds nest on the sheer vertical cliffs, and were diving into the grey sea.

The ferry turned east into Hoy Sound, and low fields replaced the stark cliffs. We saw the first Orcadian house, white, single-storeyed with slate roof. The skies cleared and the sun came out. Stone cottages, little meadows, low stone walls, yellow sand and the blue sea rolling white breakers onto the beach. We saw the wreck half-submerged between Hoy and Graemsay, and on Graemsay twin rounded hills, with the Bay of Sandside between them. Turning into Stromness Harbour, our excitement grew as the view from the stern was down Clestrain Sound and Bring Deeps, to Scapa Flow and Flotta. Suddenly we saw the oil flare in the far distance.

Quickly off the ferry, our first priority was food. A coffee shop sits at the end of the quay, and it was almost empty. By 3 p.m. we were at a corner table enjoying "broth", just 65 pence. Nothing ever tasted more delicious than this slow-cooked vegetable and beef soup with large chunks of carrot and potato. Our fingers thawed gradually, and we were glad we had brought our thick, warm jumpers. Now we were at last on Orcadian soil and could begin to relive the diary.

11. Shapinsay Tower - Balfour Castle Estate

KIRKWALL

It was evening and the wind was high. Dramatic gusts sounded thunderous. The atmosphere was once again eerie as the strike of the cathedral clock punctured the night. We were in a guest house in the centre of the Orcadian capital, and having brought our combined diaries up to date we were exhausted though contented after our first day.

We had begun with a visit to the Royal Hotel where Miss Murray stayed overnight on her way home from Flotta to Aberdeen. Large, grey, and drab, the rendered and pebble-dashed building in Victoria Street was disappointing. The new owners of six months' duration, Mr. and Mrs. Sulat, were welcoming and interested in our project. They told us what they had so far gleaned about the history of the hotel, were keen to find out more, and hoped to return the hotel to its former elegance. It would be a long job as the lounge bar was decked in black vinyl, the bedrooms in plasterboard and gaudy candlewick. Nevertheless, the view from the roof of the hotel was all we had hoped for, a layered scene of stepped gables with the Cathedral above.

St. Magnus Cathedral, commenced in 1137, is built of red and yellow sandstone, with a 20th century copper spire. Rough, now unrendered stone forms the walls of the aisles at the west end and the place is dark with low lighting. Combined with the warm, red stone, this atmosphere is welcoming. The Cathedral is like no other we have entered before. Rather than move from west to east end, foraging and reading, we absorbed instead the interior as one complete space in which the air between the columns is equally important to the columns themselves. The gloom is broken by exquisitely-coloured stained glass windows.

Eric Linklater described it thus:
'From the west door one enters, as it seems, a tall magnificence of great strength - the seven columns on each side of the nave are round and massive - and a severity that is curiously tempered by the rose-red colour of the stone, for the walls and the columns recede in a rose-tawny gloom, and soar to lighter hues under the sky's illumination of the clerestory.'*

The organist started playing soaring, uplifting music to accompany our walk round, and we approached the organ as the music came to an end. It looked modern so we asked, to be told it dates from 1925, a pipe organ by Willis of London refurbished last in 1971.

As we emerged, blinking, into the daylight, the town was bustling, busy with islanders and tourists alike. For the off-islanders, a visit to Kirkwall is a big event, frequently necessitating an overnight stay. The guest houses and cafes clearly cater for these as well as for visitors like ourselves.

After purchasing new camera batteries in "Orkney Television Enterprise" nearby where the window display advertised "Hot Summer Deals" we shivered beneath our layers and headed for the St. Magnus Cafe and a welcome coffee.

To investigate property prices and compare these with those in England, we then visited T.P. and J.L. Low, the only estate agency we had seen in Kirkwall. No sales particulars were exhibited in the reception area, and it appeared that we must give our names and

*
Orkney and Shetland, by Eric Linklater, 5th edition revised by James R. Nicolson, published by Robert Hale Ltd., 1990. Eric Linklater (1899-1974 came of an Orkney family. He travelled widely, especially in India and the United States, and was Professor of English Literature and then Rector of Edinburgh University. His works include novels, plays, verse and biography. **Orkney and Shetland** was originally published in 1965 to great acclaim and is still held as one of the foremost descriptions of the landscape and heritage of the Northern Isles.

be "seen". The sign outside had read "solicitors and estate agents", and we were curious as to how these occupations overlap. From an office emerged a gentleman resplendent in a navy Crimplene suit with lapels to the shoulders. He gave us the two sales particulars we had selected from the display in the window: a back street store for conversion in the centre of Kirkwall, offers around eight thousand pounds , and a one-roomed cottage on Stronsay, described thus,

"Lower Dishes comprises a stone cottage with garden area and outbuilding situated on the shore side at the edge of the bay, enjoying superb views, bird life and seals in the bay" - 350 square feet in all for 6,000 pounds ono.

He explained that prices are increasing throughout Orkney because southerners from Aberdeen (note!) and even from south east England are keen to buy. Yes, it is driving away young locals, but Orkney sellers welcome it with open arms and open wallets, and positively encourage him to advertise their properties in the south east.

Back into the street we saw "the tree". An old photograph taken around 1870 depicting the Big Tree of Albert Street was, for us, the beginning of a story at the centre of Kirkwall life that spans over 120 years. The tree was initially enclosed in a private garden. When the Corporation wanted to widen the street, and applied to purchase the private ground, the conditions of sale stipulated that one tree should be retained. A photograph of 1889 shows the tree, released from its garden, and part of the street scene. Looking at it in 1989 we could not believe that what was little more than a stump, with just a few meagre shoots where the crown should be, was indeed the Big Tree of Albert Street. The position was correct, and the presence of the Tree Bakery suggested that this was the important tree. But, it wasn't until later that we heard the strange further chapter in the story. In the summer of 1987, the tree was pronounced dangerous and a "maniac" from the Parks Department was let loose with a chainsaw. He cut off all the branches, and there was an outcry as the tree was thought to be dead. Orcadians are very protective of their trees, due to the sparsity; the majority are in private gardens, apart from those behind the Bishop's Palace and in front of the Cathedral. To attempt a remedy, one resident planted a Christmas tree in the hollow of the trunk so that something should grow on this site. The Council objected, however, and that tree was removed. Thankfully the original has now struggled back to life.

Our walk took us through the town, in which many streets are paved. It is not that these thoroughfares have become pedestrianised; pedestrians have always had more right of way than vehicles. Even otters are catered for with their own warning signs "otters crossing" dotted about the capital's roads. In the Tankerness House Museum in Broad Street we found an exhibition about "The First Settlers", the Vikings who came here over 5000 years ago. They settled in villages, until about 2000 BC, when the pattern changed to one of isolated farms. At approximately the same time, contact with Scotland diminished and that with Shetland increased. In one display cabinet resides a rough wooden box, identified as a discovery during restoration work in the last century within a Cathedral pillar. When opened, its contents were revealed as the bones of St. Magnus, obviously embedded in the fabric during construction, for safekeeping. Another cabinet is filled with personal artefacts, bone combs, silver and bronze brooches, and silver armlets which are thought to have been used as currency.

So closed an eventful day in the islands' capital. It is steeped in fascinating history, and St. Magnus Cathedral imparts a sense of wonder and calm.

STROMNESS

Our first view of Stromness was from the ferry. It looked an antiquated port with attractive grey buildings huddling around its harbour, and we relished the chance to explore.

The main street hardly seemed like a road at all, since it is paved with local flagstones. There is no distinction between road and pavement in any case, all is very haphazard and relaxed. In the gaps between the buildings on our left as we wandered along Victoria Street, were small alleyways leading to the water's edge. Each had at its end a view of water, boats and islands - as well as a washing line! One alley had such pretty gardens leading down to one of the private quays for which Stromness is famous. It is the sort of place where people used to fish out of their kitchen window.

This was 'Shopping Week' in Stromness and bunting decked the street. The tourist brochure described this event as a Gala Week first held 42 years ago as a joint venture by the merchants of the town to encourage trade. Always held in the third week of July, it was a happy accident that our visit coincided. In the window of Wishart Hardware Ltd. a poster revealed the promise of the week: Stonehaven Pipe Band, Norwegian Folk Dancers, Daft Raft Race, Visit of Viking Longship, Greasy Pole, Three-Legged Fancy Dress Beer Race and Grand Fireworks Display. An Evening of Music and Song featuring Logins Well at the Royal Hotel offered 'bar service' and 'informality'. Delighted with this precis, we asked if the shop had a copy of the poster to spare for us. They hadn't, but were willing to let us have this one. "It will only be thrown out on Monday, after all".

Apart from the organised events, we heard snippets of conversation indicating that 'Shopping Week' is just as much a social gathering to give family and friends far away an excuse to return. "Is your daughter coming home?"

In the Hamnavoe restaurant for lunch we found an unassuming, old-fashioned homely atmosphere. The dining room is elegant with various old tables and chairs of good quality, plates hung on cream-painted walls, and beautiful fireplaces at each end. We lingered over chilled wine and fish pates. What are Clootie Dumplings? To find out, we ordered them and discovered that they are like slices of Christmas pudding, topped with cream. Some people were having tea while others were finishing lunch, and this lent a relaxed, unhurried tone to the day. We indulged in a second glass of wine. In a bi-monthly journal, *The Orkney View,* lying nearby, we read a poem entitled 'Graduation Grumbles' in which a university student bemoaned time spent away from the islands,

"An' a peedie bit o' Prof said:
'Where a man sows, there he reaps'
But I'd rather be in Orkney
Singlan' neeps"

Further up Victoria Street we reached the famous Pier Arts Centre. The temporary exhibition was the work of William G. Thomson, an elderly man from North Ronaldsay, whose artistic career began late in life. His subjects are ships, painted on canvas, bottles and floats - quite 'naive' art except for the very clever detailing of the rigging. The permanent exhibition is modern art and neither of us was sure we would appreciate it. The first piece was not encouraging: nine 'blobs' - three brown, three white, three grey, arranged in rows.

Our difficulties were compounded by the fact that the guide book gave only titles of paintings and names of the artists. In some cases the title revealed uncertainty in the artist himself, as in 'Roger Hilton, c. 1958: boat, perhaps?' Nevertheless, forging on, we both found pieces we liked. Barbara Hepworth's sculptures appealed to Anne, particularly the 'Figure in Sycamore, 1931'. Jacqueline savoured for a considerable time Calum Colvin's 'Incubus'.

In the open courtyard there was the music of a Country and Western band, clearly a 'Shopping Week' event. Finding the work of Barbara Hepworth and Ben Nicholson so far north had seemed surprising enough, but even more so against these American sounds. The paving stones, as we walked, were brightly coloured with chalk drawings by Orcadian children.

Our guest house was a short distance, conveniently situated opposite the Ferry Inn on the edge of the harbour. Our second floor twin room had every comfort: rose-patterned white bedlinen with lace, two Orkney chairs, two hot water bottles with pink jackets, and a sky light looking across the misty rooftops, through to the St. Ola at her berth. Also provided were cotton wool buds, sea sickness pills, sewing and shoe-cleaning kits, tissues, kitchen roll, fresh fruit, hairdryer....We collapsed gratefully onto our beds to write our diaries. Later, crossing to the Ferry Inn and securing a table in the busy, noisy and quite smoky interior, we continued writing until our meal arrived.

A ship's loud foghorn awakened us the next morning at seven. Down the staircase festooned with colourful silk flowers, the dining room was a splendid combination of styles: Swedish sauna, Aladdin's cave, and a hint of the Fairy Grotto. A deer's head marked the entrance. Until we read the napkins, which spelled out Good Morning in pink, it was hard to believe that it was 8.30 a.m. Red lamps, silver napkin rings, coasters and toothpick holders, orange juice served in tall stemmed glasses, each with plastic cocktail stick balanced on the top, holding an orange slice and glace cherry, plastic ice cubes, suggested to us that the owners subscribed to *The Landlady* or some such magazine, and sent off for all the offers. In addition, instrumental muzak played and played and drove us up the (red velvet) wall. Our haddock, chosen from nine other possibilities, arrived on fish-shaped plates. The Austrian-style cuckoo clock struck the hour at 5 to 9....

12. Fara Church with oil terminal in background

TO FLOTTA AND THE MANSE

The 'Hoy Head' edged through the foam toward us. We stood on the quay, buffeted by winds and watched the waves breaking over the end of the pier, sick with dread at the prospect of crossing in such a storm. The ferry has an open middle for vehicles, and to the right side a narrow enclosed passage with steps leading down into a passenger lounge. Out on the bow to take photographs, the ferryman shooed us back inside, explaining they must lock the doors as the waves would break over the bows! To our relief, however, the stern door of the passageway was left open and we stood just outside it, protected by a canopy. Never had a boat trip been so enjoyable. Neither of us felt the least bit queasy. The wave crests were level with the side of the boat, and when a torrent rushed over the deck we leapt onto the step to avoid the wash, praying our boots wouldn't leak. The single fare of one pound forty pence was well spent, for the pleasure of feeling the salt spray on our faces. The ferryman remarked that the gale was Force 7 to 8. The fine spray moistened our faces and our lungs filled with the coldest, freshest air imaginable, leaving us gasping to catch our breath.

The boat drew near to Flotta and reaching for our bags, we heard a crew member saying, "This is Flotta", as if we couldn't be disembarking here, but should be staying on for Lyness in Hoy. But, Phyllis was waiting as the ferry docked, and drove us to the Manse.

For us, the arrival passed in a dream-like idyll. The Manse is a solid T-shaped house of stone, standing tall and proud. Its setting captivated us completely, as it overlooks Kirk Bay, on the southern side of the island, and is no more than 200 yards from the water. Not only does it take in the full sweep of the bay but also looks to the church with its walled graveyard and across the patchwork quilt of fields. The small isle of Switha beyond the bay is also part of the scene.

We passed through the unlocked front door and into a light, airy and immaculately decorated home. Phyllis had prepared a large bedroom for each of us, but we decided to share the twin room where windows overlook the bay on one side and the church on the other. These views are like paintings on the wall, the windows acting as frames.

While we sat by the kitchen Aga talking about our journey so far, Phyllis prepared a ham and egg salad. Phyllis could not have known, not having the opportunity as yet to read the diary, that Miss Murray was also served ham and eggs on arrival at the Manse. We laughed and explained the coincidence. On the table apart from the salad were rolls, bread, crackers, cheese, jams, home-made cakes and rice biscuits. Through the kitchen window we could see the oil flare - Phyllis remarked that they don't like to see the flame horizontal as it is today.

After tea we began to hear about the renovation of the Manse and to see photographs of the re-building stages. Phyllis produced a copy of the original specification (1892) and modern photographs of the several builders and their work who came for many weeks to complete the restoration from a state of near collapse. When Reverend Mitchell, with whom Miss Murray stayed, arrived in Flotta in 1884, the Manse was a small stone building closer to the church. He campaigned to raise funds for building a new Manse, and this resulted in the 1892 plans with a detailed specification running to 30 pages of close handwriting. Having these in hand we were able to see the whole of the building at the drawing board stage, and read about features still present like the four-panelled doors.

Details of the plumbing are fascinating: the cistern of Welsh slate, the 'Simplicities' wash-down closet (manufactured by Doulton and Co., London) with pine seat, brackets, chain pull and ornamental basin, list price 3.10/- sterg. Also a brass force pump in the kitchen with suction pipe to the well; the specification requires that a quote be made 'for sinking and building a well say 10 ft. by 3 ft., properly covered in stone.' Phyllis has no knowledge of a well, so we are unsure whether or not this was constructed.

The entire house was to be superbly embellished: 'The walls of the Parlour and Dining room will be hung with paper @ 2/6 p.roll; the walls of four bedrooms will be hung with paper @ 8/-p.roll.' This seemed something of a contrast with modern-day priorities when generally bedrooms would be decorated with cheaper wallpaper. 'All paper patterns are to be selected by the Minister or Architect.' Six servants' bells were to be hung on a board in the kitchen; each with vibrating pendulum attached; part of a sophisticated system which included maple mounting on the levers in the parlour and bedroom, and ebony in the dining room.

Still in place at the core of the house is the staircase, so wonderfully described: 'Build in the stair on 1 1/4" wall stringers with 1 1/4" bottled treads, 7/8" risers, ends returned as brackets over wall stringers, and plant moulding along plaster. The ballusters to be Falkirk pattern, with newel, set in screwed and sunk overhanging brackets, two to each full step, batted in lead. The tops rivetted to 3/4" dble nailed iron hoop, and surmounted with a 2 1/2" x 1 3/4" checked oval pitchpine handrail dowelled and bolted at Joints with scroll at bottom and all proper ramps and turns as necessary and cleaned for varnish.'

We admire Phyllis for her inspiration and determination in renovating the Manse. We both warmed to her immediately and felt totally at ease in her company. She is dark-haired, small and slight, a gentle and caring person. She knows her own mind, and at her core is a tough spirit. Many Orcadians appear to take their holidays in Europe, and Phyllis has travelled even more widely, journeying farther afield to India and Egypt. Quite the opposite from inward-looking or insular as we might have expected a 'Flottarian' to be, she had many more travel anecdotes and tales to tell than the two of us put together!

13. Stones of Stenness

14. Stone dresser, Skara Brae

THE POST OFFICE

On the shore of Pan Hope nestles Lairdy, and opposite, across the water is the oil terminal. Lairdy, with its huddle of outbuildings, is now Flotta's Post Office and shop. There the white-painted shelves from floor to ceiling are crammed with a colourful array of tins, tubes, packets and bottles. Now the only shop on the island, it sells everything from Wellington boots to video films, and tinned ham to kiwi fruit. What it doesn't have in stock can be sent over on the ferry at a brief telephone call. The shop is the hub of Flotta's day-to-day social life, where everyone goes to tell and hear all the news. With no set opening hours, Marina Sinclair opens in the morning with the first knock on the door - usually about 9 a.m. - and closes when the last customer goes home at about 9 p.m. With no lunchtime closing - and often a burnt dinner - it is a long day. Evening is also a social occasion; the islanders tend to shop in the evening because the 'mails' and the newspapers come on the 5 p.m. ferry. Otherwise they would have to wait until the next day to receive them.

At Lairdy, we met Phyllis' father, David Sinclair. Dressed in a blue boiler suit, bearing the words 'Auxiliary Coastguard', he had just returned from a cliff rescue practice. We already knew from Phyllis that he ran the Post Office and was the island's Registrar. Here was a man in the best tradition of the highlands and islands, who held a variety of jobs. We were reminded of the popular Scottish film of late, 'Local Hero', and asked if he had even more occupations. Oh, yes - Burial Ground Clerk, Calor Gas Supplier, operator of the island's only petrol pump, Justice of the Peace, unofficial taxi driver - and he keeps sheep. He would have been the Welfare Officer for Flotta, but believed there would be a clash of interests and a possible lack of confidentiality. He used to play the accordian in the local dance band, but gradually this dispersed, and visiting bands are now brought in. Before the oil came, his list of jobs was even longer, as he was postman, Chairman of the local Community Council and kept cattle too. Now a main occupation is harassing the Orkney Islands Council on all matters concerning Flottarian and Orcadian life, about which he feels strongly. In short, he acts as a fulcrum of the community, keeping all in balance.

We took to David straightaway and liked him immensely. He is one of those people who, when he enters a room, seems to breathe life into any gathering. Insiders and outsiders look to him with respect for his opinions and advice. He was kind to us, and anxious to show us everything of note on Flotta. Already he had taken us to see the 'Cletts' and the 'Gloups', cliff rock formations which are home to many wild flowers and nesting sea birds. We also saw seals, like Miss Murray, and the gyral's house, a roofless cave whose inhabitant is said to be a legendary black-horned monster. David was, nevertheless, apologetic, "Flotta does not have much in the way of tourist attractions". We demurred; Flotta does not have tourists!

Invited to Sunday lunch at Lairdy, Marina had prepared for us a delicious home-made vegetable broth, followed by roast pork, new potatoes (she complained that although labelled Orkney 'tatties', they obviously were not as these did not scrape well) and mashed cauliflower, with jelly, fruit salad and ice cream to finish. The number of places laid at table was one short, and indeed after waiting on us all, Marina ate her lunch seated on a chair by the kitchen door - on the other side of the room. Samples of David's wit punctuated the meal. As we were late in arriving at Lairdy from church, the broth was less than hot, causing David to remark out of Marina's hearing: "the soup is cold but it's no' safe to complain". His version of the famous "Stromness is the Venice of the North", was "Of course, Venice is the Stromness of the South". We learned that his sense of humour is known far and wide, partly through a series of Radio Orkney April Fool broadcasts. One notorious example involved a plague of squirrels which was eating through all the island's greenery (there are no squirrels in Orkney). A man from the Forestry Commission telephoned David, desperate to help, genuinely amazed that squirrels could cause such widespread damage. David hadn't the heart to explain the hoax. Another year's prank caused more widespread ire. A new car ferry was about to be introduced and David pre-empted this by broadcasting that it would berth at Scapa Bay (where the pier has no ramp suitable for vehicles) rather than at Houton, where a new pier with ramp had been built. A number of people turned up for the new ferry at Scapa Bay, and the shipping company had to bear the brunt from irate callers.

When David read Miss Murray's account in the 1900 diary of the weekly visit to the floating shop, he explained his own rather tongue-in-cheek plan for a similar venture which could be transformed into a disco boat by night. This idea, he was sure, could be put to the Orkney Islands Council which apparently 'has tried to use the oil revenues to help new enterprises get started.'

The writer in David - apart from all his other occupations - has come forward under the well-known appellation and pseudonym of 'Willick o' Pirliebraes', the derivation of which must be explained. Due to his numerous past letters to The Orcadian newspaper, he decided on the anonymity of a fictitious name, which eventually attained almost a cult-following. Willick grew to embody the archetypal islander. Orcadian custom adds the tag 'ick' to the first syllable of the forename, and men are known by the place in which they reside, so actually David Sinclair is 'Davick o'Lairdy'. But, as an author, Willick he became and 'Pirliebraes' his fictitious home. Encouraged to write an entire book around this character who consolidated the worst and darkest aspects of Flottarian life, his best selling book was simply called *'Willick o' Pirliebraes'.* *

*   Published by The Orkney Press, July, 1981.

The Post Master's private office at the Post Office is a treasure trove - a tiny room piled high with four types of whisky, three of rum, McEwan's Pale Ale, Coca Cola cans to the ceiling. The sorting office pigeon holes, labelled variously 'Hungerhimout' and 'Stanstanes' (Standing Stones) line one wall. A cassette recorder, a word processor, safe, CB radio, the desk from the old post office all sit together in a glorious jumble. He let us have a try at postmarking our own mail, but it is a practised art. People come from all over to obtain a Flotta postmark, just as 'Island Baggers' also come here to collect the stamp on their passports. The whole of Flotta has the same postcode - KW16 3NP.

All the old registers, birth and death, reside in the Post Office. The Deaths registers begin in 1859, when registration first became compulsory in Scotland. The third entry in this first volume is that of Davick's great great grandmother who died of consumption, aged 41. The 1900 Deaths register includes the names of some of the seriously ill whom Miss Murray visited with Reverend Mitchell during her stay. Six consecutive entries for that summer of 1900 show a long-lived people, ages ranging from 65 to 85. Davick explained that when people died young, it was usually either consumption (tuberculosis) or drowning (especially if drunk). Most Flottarians cannot swim. There is no swimming pool and the sea is invariably too cold.

Mrs. Mitchell's death, 22 years after Miss Murray stayed with them in the Manse, is registered on 4th August, 1922 at 5.30 a.m. The oldest register held on Flotta is the Baptismal one for 1771, an extremely fragile set of tattered pages with faded ink. *Peace's Almanack and County Directory (Orkney and Shetland Edition)* for 1910 shows us that the population of Flotta was 431, and included two blacksmiths, four carpenters, three dressmakers, two masons, four merchants, two shoemakers, a tailor, teacher, doctor, minister and, of course, a postmaster.

We left the Post Office-cum-shop for the house, a short walk, and Phyllis's grandmother, Hope, was sitting in an upright chair to one side of the fire. 'Cat', a mottled tortoiseshell, and Skip, the dog, were skirmishing over the bean bag on the other. When the glass door on the stove was opened we saw the burning peats - oblong blocks about 8" x 8" x 2". That batch took four and a half weeks to dry.

Davick and Marina were amused to see their table strewn with the objects we collected on our walks: urchins, winkles, wool and stones, wild flowers, cotton and shells. As she set the plates of 'home-bakes' and mugs of coffee among the clutter, Marina asked us to take a photograph of her tea table, as "it had never looked like this before". Davick gave us bits of peat to add to our collection, then disappeared to fetch plastic bags for our 'samples'.

"You will get used to the strange Orkney eating habits", Phyllis said. By that she meant that the main meal is eaten at lunch time, followed by late afternoon 'tea' consisting of rolls, jam, cheese and the 'home-bakes' (slabs of home-made cake, iced sponges, chocolate cake, gingerbread and fruit cake). A late supper is then served at around 11 p.m.: sweet and savoury biscuits, shortbread, and more home-bakes. The latter is predominantly sweet, rather than savoury.

ISLANDERS

One evening gathered round the peat fire at Lairdy in the company of Phyllis, her family and Mary Fortnum, became a most memorable occasion. In those few hours we began to 'feel' the character of the islanders.

Mary Fortnum was born on 10 September 1900, a fact which instantly revealed the unexplained reasons for Mrs. Mitchell's disappearances from church that summer. She was, of course, expecting her first child in two months' time, and Mary, now 92 years of age and fit and well, is that child. In the diary, Mrs. Mitchell's delicate condition was clearly a taboo subject. Mary was thrilled to see the diary for the first time, and the evening gradually became a reading, with Davick and Mary giving the recital between them, until the whole history had been heard.

The reading was broken only with Mary's comments which prompted Hope to enter the reminiscing. The two have been friends for most of their lives, despite separation when Mary spent many years in Canada, and it's obvious that they could chat endlessly about times past. In an island community where everyone knows everyone else and many intermarry, the discussions inevitably centre on families and someone's sister. George Mackay Brown says of the Norse habit of recording great lineages as a prelude to the Sagas:
'This gift has come down in all its essentials to certain modern Orkney men and women; you have simply to name a person in the presence of these 'kin-redders', and they will immediately surround that name with cousins, step-brothers....'*

---

*   **Portrait of Orkney** by George Mackay Brown, Orkney's most famous writer. Published by The Hogarth Press, London, 1981.

Reading about Jacobina, Mary recalled that her surname was Robertson and that her mother was ill for 20 years before she died. It was recalled that Mr. Mitchell played the fiddle, and that the small boat which he used to cross Calf Sound to Flotta Calf was made by an islander, Tom Sutherland. Carlo was a large black dog which Mary remembered from her youth. She was the only one who gave him his medicine, and loved him more than any dog since. Finally he had to be put down, and was shot as was the custom then. For years afterwards Mary cried at the mention of his name. When Mary read from the diary, 'The Post Office.....is of a very primitive appearance, compared to those in the South', Marina responded drily, 'The Post Office hasna changed any!'

We had half-expected that Mary might find it strange or even sad reading about her parents. Instead, her smile and her fascination with the diary, and her reading, gave us a key unlocking the Mitchell family from the pages of Miss Murray's diary. At 11 p.m. Marina served the customary Orkney supper of home-bakes, shortbread and biscuits, but perhaps in our and Mary's honour, there was also savoury fare in the form of ham pate rolls. An unforgettable evening unfolded to us in front of the peat fire on the tiny windswept island of Flotta. Finding it hard to absorb the range and depth and complexity of our feelings, and even more difficult to express those in a diary of our own, we know that it will remain vividly in our minds for the rest of our lives.

Since the death of her husband, Hope Sinclair (nee Sutherland) doesn't like to be left in her house alone. Each night at eight o'clock she is fetched to the Post Office where she spends night and morning. With Phyllis we drove to collect 'Granny' who waited outside in the rain with coat, bag and walking stick. Once at Lairdy she sat in her fireside chair, in silence, hands clasped in her lap. With talk of the past, she was stirred to delve into a suitcase full of old photographs, and to relate animatedly stories from her younger days. Of particular significance to us was a clear, though tattered, photograph of sheep-shearing on Flotta Calf. From the dress it appears to have been taken around the turn of the century, and is therefore an almost direct illustration from Miss Murray's diary.

Each evening Rowland Hill Barnett calls into the Post Office to collect his mail and newspaper, leaning against the counter and talking with the other customers as they come and go. Until three years ago, when he asked Davick to take over from him, he was the island's Registrar. His name is an example of the Orcadian custom where a baby's middle name is frequently the surname of the delivering doctor; in Rowland's case, Dr. Hill. Rowland kindly produced for us photographs which included some of the Mitchell family, with the Rev. and Mrs. Mitchell, their four children, Mary, Norna, William and Charles (the one with the curly hair), their servant, Jessie Taylor, and Carlo. Like all the islanders we met, Rowland was as friendly as could be, and allowed us to borrow his photographs in order to make copies.

Sandy Flett arrived at Lairdy during Sunday lunch. He is a small, wiry man with a lined, leathery brown face, very animated and jovial, with bright eyes and a shock of white false teeth. Oblivious to the fact that we were eating our meal, he settled himself on the settee and gabbled constantly at twice the speed of sound in a broad, swerving accent. His words were totally incomprehensible to us, but he had heard of our arrival and thought we were from Australia. Davick winked at us and we played along, assuring him that we were from Wogga Wogga, until everyone was convulsed with laughter. Once it was established that we were from Devon, Sandy exclaimed 'England!', as if it were even farther away than Australia.

We learned fast about Flottarians. On our first day a farmer stopped his hay baler in mid-field to jump down and greet us with a cheery hello. "You must be the two ladies chasing up that old diary!" The accent is fascinating, and we quickly realised that it is almost without Scottish sound. Edinburgh seemed a long way away. Rather the mixture is one of Scandinavian, a little Scots and possibly Geordie. Orcadians are basically Vikings from the north who in the Middle Ages and later began to realise that in practical terms their fatherland was too far away and that the kingdom to the south could be more useful. Hence, the Scottish element in speech is a relatively new thing.

We asked Phyllis if Orcadian people feel Scottish, an important question for us since they seem far less like the people across the Pentland Firth than we had anticipated. Mistakenly we believed that Orcadians referred to their principal island as 'Mainland', but Phyllis corrected this. It is called 'The Mainland' and Scotland is 'Across the Firth'. She would give her nationality as Orcadian in preference to Scottish, but she does feel British, and these views seem typical. Some 20 years ago, there was an attempt to become part of Norway, but this was unsuccessful. The Norway-Orkney Friendship Association thrives, and its activities are akin to those of a twinning association. Perhaps the only time Orcadians look south to Scotland is when Scotland play England at football.

15. Veantrow Bay, Shapinsay

A WALK AROUND THE ISLAND

A warm sunny morning presented us with an ideal day for our walk around Flotta. We left the Manse and walked the short distance along the lane to the shore, between fields of golden buttercups and tall grasses whispering in the breeze. We sat, sheltered from the north-westerly wind, soaking up the warmth of the sun, on a pebble beach near a seaweed-covered outcrop. The only sounds were the wind rushing in the long grasses along the shore, the cries of the gulls and terns, the gentle slurp of the ebb and flow, washing the seaweed around the rocks.

Making our way up the lane, we passed through a patchwork quilt of small fields bordered by old stone walls and rickety fences with cottages at intervals, some inhabited, some tumbledown and roofless. In one newly-mown hayfield, red-beaked oystercatchers, and curlews with long hooked bills, were busily foraging and feeding. There are no trees, but the landscape was nevertheless beautiful. At the corner of each field, the lane turns a right angle. There are no meandering country roads. The lanes are narrow but strictly follow the grid pattern of the fields, so any car journey is a series of zig-zag steps. The two main roads, the B9045 and the B9046, are wide enough for two-way traffic but are really just lanes.

On the subject of cars, we learned that on Flotta the driving laws differ, both from the Mainland Orkney and the rest of Britain. There are in Orkney no traffic lights in any case, but on Flotta there is also no MOT test, seat belts are not generally worn, and provisional licence holders may drive unaccompanied. Flottarian cars of late, however, have improved in their general state of repair, since if they are taken by ferry to the Mainland, they must be at least, presentable. No cars are locked, and the fact that houses are also not locked seems to give the people of Flotta an enviable sense of freedom.

We skirted the wartime ruins on Stanger Head and negotiated a steep path down a grass and flower-strewn cliff until at the edge, we saw the Cletts, two offshore stacks of stones, one anvil-shaped and one a smaller 'Old Man of Hoy'. Puffins, also called sea-parrots or tammy-norries, nesting on the Cletts, flew around us, showing their strange little faces, mostly made up of bright orange beak. These are sometimes known locally as 'Flotta penguins', because some oil terminal construction workers seeing them for the first time, mistakenly told everyone they had seen penguins. Cormorants (scarfs) flew low over the water and the gulls wheeled and called all around. Nearby are the Gloups, two holes in the cliff with boiling surf at the bottom, collapsed caves perhaps. The turf was a carpet of wild flowers: clover, sea campion, bird's foot trefoil and vetch.

A short walk across the heather moor brought us to a small bay opposite Hoxa Head. Sitting on the heather bank, we noticed some thirty or forty seals basking on the shoreline beneath us. They varied greatly in size and colour, some dark, slate grey, others almost white with pale grey mottling. They are inquisitive and at our arrival several slipped into the water and came swimming across the bay towards us. They didn't come ashore, but remained, bobbing in the water below us, their huge, moist, sunken eyes and marvellously human, intelligent expressions beaming up at us. We were told later that before the mystery virus of 1988, it was not unusual to see 200 to 300 in this bay alone.

Later, as we picked our way over the slippery, limpet-covered rocks, we suddenly came upon a baby seal, some two feet long, lying camouflaged among the rocks. We looked anxiously towards the water in anticipation of an angry mother, but the seals watching from the shallows gazed on impassively. The young seal looked ill, lying partly on its side, panting slightly, and now and then wearily laying its head down on the rocks with eyes closed. All that we could do was pass by quickly so as to cause it least distress, and it remained unalarmed, turning its head and craning its neck to watch us.

In Miss Murray's diary she refers to the sport of seal-shooting, though her 1951 postscript confirms her subsequent abhorrence of any killing of animals. We heard of islanders who were afraid of seals, of their big, strange, almost human eyes. Superstition surrounds them. If a seal surfaces next to a boat, some believe it to be an ancestor returned, and name the seal accordingly.

The weather was kind for our walk although during our visit the temperature was only around 50 degrees F, whilst the south-west of England sweltered in sizzling temperatures of 90 degrees or more. Phyllis immediately apologised for the weather when we first stepped ashore on a grey and stormy Flotta, describing it as poor even by their own summer standards, and more like Orkney November squalls. Although windy throughout our stay, only twice was it 'raining in torrents' as described by Miss Murray, and we were not subjected to the infamous 'Force 9 Fog', that is gale and fog together. They say, 'if you can survive the Orkney summer, you'll be okay come winter, as they're much the same.'

Passing the green waters of Pan Hope, the spaghetti jumble of shiny pipes and tanks of all shapes and sizes at the terminal, and the roaring flare, we reached the Golta peninsula. The ground cover is low, no shrubs or trees, but the now-familiar blend of heather, clover and wild cotton. Rabbits were everywhere, and we learned that these have inherited their varied colours - white, ginger, black - from the years of World War II when someone brought pet rabbits which escaped or were let loose. Farther on again we passed the excavated tip where Flotta's refuse is buried, and saw strips of land from where peat had been cut. Dozens of terns were wheeling and diving overhead. They nest there but peat-cutting time coincides with their breeding and they can be vicious when disturbed.

Peat rights are ancient and frequently disputed. During our visit we saw a job vacancy advertised in The Orcadian for a clerk to research peat rights at Gaitnip on the Mainland. Inhabitants of one island may hold peat rights on another. And this fact comes close to the bone for Flotta, where the inhabitants of South Ronaldsay (having no peat) have rights to cut. In the past, when they tried to exercise these rights, their boats were pelted with stones as they rounded Stanger Head by Flottarians who didn't believe that peat should be cut by outsiders.

Returning to the Manse, we lingered a while in the lane to collect some of the grasses and wild flowers from the verge. Spreading them out on Phyllis' kitchen table, we found we had a wide variety which included buttercups, pink and white clovers, celandines, dandelions, vetches and daisies. Pressing these onto cards in a variety of styles and designs, we passed some relaxing hours. And later, showing them to Davick, Marina and some Post Office customers, we were pleased that they found the cards so attractive. Marina seemed astonished, "You would not believe these have come from the roadside - we never give them a second look." We realised, of course, that they lead such busy working lives there that they barely have time to notice the exquisite flora all around.

FLOTTA CHURCH

On Sunday we attended church, as Miss Murray had done in her time. It is a short distance along the lane from Phyllis' house, and our view as we walked was of the low-walled graveyard next to the shore. Within the graveyard's perimeter and along one side stands the little church, not the traditional English parish church of stone and spire, but a pale, rendered building of square proportions, plain but neat and attractive.

There are two sections to the graveyard. Recently a new area has been walled off, adjacent to the old. We entered the older part through a wrought iron gate and walked slowly round. The gravestones stand starkly, surrounded by flat, cropped turf. Many are of white stone and reflected the milky sunlight piercing the heavy grey clouds. A white cross, more brightly-lit than any other, drew our attention and it marked the grave of Mrs. Mitchell. The inscription reads:

Sacred to the memory of Elizabeth Amy Mitchell.
Wife of the Rev. A A Mitchell.
Parish Minister of Flotta and Phara
Aged 53 years.
For nearly 23 years she was the accomplished organist

Many graves are lichen-covered, and the same few family names predominate: Sutherland, Flett, Sabiston, Simpson, Mowat.

We climbed the steps, entered the church and contributed to the collection plate by the door, already brimming with Scottish pound notes. Entering the main room, we found ourselves in a single, uninterrupted space, without pillars. Long wooden pews range the width of the building and there is no central aisle. A small communion table is in the centre at the front. Behind it, facing the congregation, is the organ and organist, and behind that, a wooden pulpit, with steps up to it and a separate, wall-mounted, conical canopy. In the east wall are two stained glass windows, one of St. Paul, and one depicting the Good Shepherd.

The interior is painted a pale duck-egg blue, with a thin red border edging the window recesses. On one window sill sat a potted geranium, a recent addition by Christine Rosie, a member of the Congregational Board, and put there before she, or anyone there, knew that the church was so decorated with geraniums in 1900. Another vestige of Miss Murray's description is the crimson organ cloth, with its embroidery of white lilies. Naturally the cloth has needed replacing over the years, but each time the embroidery has been carefully transferred to the new fabric.

At 10.45 we took our seats with Phyllis and about twenty others, leaving many pews empty. Apart from one lady and three children in the front row, everyone else sat in the back three rows. The locum doctor's wife, Mrs. Ross, told us the amusing story, that when she asked why the back row was so popular, the reply was that "it's the 'nit row'". No-one is able to sit behind you and see the lice in your hair. Mrs. Ross sits three rows forward, but tradition prevails and most like to sit at the back.

The first hymn was No. 39, 'Stand Up and Bless the Lord', pitched in a key too high for the congregation and played very slowly. Christine Rosie read the lesson, Ephesians 6: 10-20, 'Put on the armour of God', from the New English Bible. We sang 'Jesus Loves Me, This I Know', No. 418 and three further hymns : No. 139, Psalm 121, 'I to the Hills Will Lift Mine Eyes', No. 677, 'O Love That Wilt Not Let Me Go' and No. 477, 'Rise Up, O Men of God'.

Like the reading, the sermon was based on Ephesians 6, 10-20. Reverend W. Graham Monteith is, despite crippling cerebral palsy, extremely articulate. There was no communion. The Church of Scotland celebrates this only twice yearly, in May and November, on no specific notable date in the church calendar. After the service, Phyllis introduced us to the Minister. Wishing us well with our project, he confirmed that we could take photographs inside the church, and then took us to see the Bible, with its inscription handwritten in ink:

Presented to the Kirk-Session and Congregation of Flotta Parish Church q.s., as the Pulpit Bible by the First Minister of the Church and Parish, Revd. Alexander Arnot Mitchell. Easter 1908.

16. Sheep-shearing at Fara

FARA AND CALF OF FLOTTA

For Sunday lunch at the Manse we were joined by a friend of Phyllis, Kenny Gee. He works at the terminal, travelling over each day from his home in Orphir on the Mainland. Having promised to take us to Fara and Flotta Calf in his speedboat, he decided that today the sea was sufficiently calm for our trip.

Miss Murray's description of sheep shearing on Flotta Calf has stayed with us and although it was not taking place at that time on the Calf, we decided to visit in order to see where it all happened. Then on to Fara, where Kenny was told there was a shearing that very day. We were most fortunate to see it at all because it was late in the farming calendar for shearing.

The wind rose, and although the sea was still fairly calm, the crossing to Fara was bumpy. We were covered in spray and attempted to move with the boat as if riding horses. After punting the boat in as far as he could, Kenny carried his three female passengers safely to shore by piggy-back. We thought of Tess and Angel Clare, Retty, Marian and Izz on their way to church in Thomas Hardy's rural story. Seals were further along the shore, and they all dropped into the water with an unison splash at our approach.

As we crossed the beach, which was a mass of small pyramids, each topped with a large worm-cast (lugworms), the air was ringing with the pitiful bleating of lambs separated from their mothers. On the way toward the sheep cries, we visited the old church, now deserted. In Miss Murray's words, 'After landing on the shore of Fara, we had not far to walk to the church. It is a mission church and is a very nice compact, little building, which is seated to hold about 120.' Peering inside we disturbed two pigeons, one of which flew through a window shattering the glass. Collecting up the glass to save the feet of sheep, we found a half-open sash window and climbed through. It was a tiny room and we couldn't imagine how it seated 120. The whole place was carpeted with bird droppings and in an adjacent room we discovered the old stone cross that presumably used to stand on the gable end. Outside again, we looked at Miss Murray's account of the service at Fara Church, and found that she had heard on that day the same reading we had heard in Flotta Church this morning: St. Paul's Epistle to the Ephesians 6th ch. part of the 17th vr.

Finally we reached the tumbledown farm on the summit of Fara, where a dozen or so people were busy shearing. A couple of men were 'feeding' the sheep along a narrow corridor between two solid metal barricades, a couple were shearing with electric clippers, two girls were spreading out, smoothing and then rolling the fleeces. The fleeces, then, were passed to another man atop a large oblong plastic bag - 6 feet long by 5 feet high - into which he was stuffing them and treading them down.

One man was videoing the shearing and to one side two older, weatherbeaten men were castrating the male lambs. One by one, each lamb was laid on the table and held down by one of the men while the other castrated, by means of a large pair of pliers, then inoculated. Phyllis said that castration these days is not literal. They merely cut off the blood supply by applying pressure to the blood vessels. They do sometimes make mistakes but overall the procedure is still "more humane than Rowland with his knife". The workers then took a break, and brought out cans of lager; not quite the 1900 'stone jars of porter'.

Heading back to the boat, we saw flocks of terns wheeling overhead. Kenny said they are now an endangered species because of overfishing of their food, sand eels. We combed the beach for a few more samples and collected some periwinkles and fragments of spiky urchins, smashed by hungry birds' beaks. The boat was tied up at the end of a jetty which Phyllis told us was built at the same time as the church, so Miss Murray would have disembarked here.

The swell was about four feet, and when Kenny saw a high wave ahead, he rode it, so that the boat was at a 45 degree angle to the water. The sheep ran up the cliffs from the beach as we approached Flotta Calf, and jumping ashore, we were faced with what seemed an impossible, slippery mass of rocks and seaweed. Our feet disappeared into wet voids between the rocks, and it was only due to Kenny's help that we could cross it at all. Then it became a matter of scaling the sheep tracks up a cliff until we reached the top with great relief.

Flotta Calf is flat-topped, a small uninhabited island without a building of any kind. In parts it is fern-covered and the remainder is grassy, close-cropped by the sheep. The surface of the land is riddled with rabbit runs and we almost expected the ground to collapse beneath us as frightened rabbits scampered away.

It was now too rough to go back to the pier so Kenny took us south down Scapa Flow. We saw about twenty seals on a beach and they dived into the water to swim inquisitively toward the boat. Kenny slowed to avoid frightening them, and we could see their shiny, silky heads and deep-set eyes at close quarters. We went ashore at the ruined pier in Pan Hope, adjacent to the old (now derelict) post office. Lobster pots, or creels, were stacked on the pier and walking along the beach to Lairdy we collected more shells and rocks with remarkable swirl patterns.

We returned to the Manse, full of our memorable afternoon experiences, and collapsed gratefully into steaming hot baths. The water is soft, but brown. Flotta's water comes from Hoy, and it is probably the peat which makes the water orangey-brown in colour.

OIL

In the mid-seventies Flotta was invaded by a force that would change life on the island forever. This is a controversial statement, as The Elf Enterprise Consortium is proud to claim that it has not harmed Flotta. Though we believe this to be true, it is obvious that the siting of a major oil processing terminal here could not go unnoticed. The islanders still go about their daily life in much the same way, and few have even seen round the terminal, but it is often referred to in conversation. We regularly heard "before the oil..." and "after the oil...".

The Sinclair family has been closely involved all along. Phyllis worked for one of the contractors during the construction phase and is now in the Employee Relations Department at Elf. Davick was Chairman of the Community Council for much of the construction phase, and became an important 'voice', representing the interests of the islanders. He and Marina came to know many of the construction workers, as dozens of Irishmen, and men from all parts arrived; these were the 'Flotta Bears' as they were known. On pay day, the Royal Bank of Scotland visited the terminal, as it still does, and the Post Office was never busier. The contractors collected their weekly wages and headed straight to Lairdy to send cash home by registered post. After a time, the Sinclairs set up a counter at the terminal to deal with this routine each Thursday afternoon.

At a public meeting all the islanders but two voted in favour of the terminal. One exception was Phyllis, then sixteen years old. Her vote didn't count because she was 'too young' but she hasn't forgotten, "I didn't want Elf here - Flotta was mine". At the time a crucial issue was the doctor, since the resident doctor had been withdrawn due to 'lack of demand'. A district nurse was in residence, and a doctor came from Hoy once a week and in case of emergency. This was tolerated until the district nurse went to Hoy to marry the doctor, when neither was replaced. The proposed terminal would mean having a full time doctor in residence once more, and this was, therefore, a positive influence.

Environmentally, Elf has changed the island very little. The company won several awards in 1982 for outstanding efforts made to reduce the visual impact of the terminal and to safeguard the marine environment. These were the Business and Industry Panel for the Environment Gold Award, the Civic Trust Award, and the Award of the Association for the Protection of Rural Scotland. The tanks and towers are visible only from geographically high points on the island, such as from Stanger Head. The main reminder of the terminal is the flare which served as our guiding light on the way to Flotta. Phyllis described the first day the flare was lit, 26 December, 1976, when it had snowed much more than usual and the whole of the island was white. The flare was lit and a strange orange glow tinted the white blanket.

After much planning, the tanks were set low and the earth landscaped around them. This meant that Elf had to install deep well pumps to push the oil to the loading pumps and then to the tankers. The tanks are a browny-green shade, expecially chosen as the least conspicuous after a year-long study of the local vegetation, light quality, and weather. The land on which the terminal is built was mainly farmland and scrubland. The occupied farms of Little Blowmuir and Netherhouse were lost. The Sutherland brothers, who farmed at Whanclett, sold readily and the family now split the year between the Mainland and Flotta, so that they still fish as much as they like. Housca, referred to so much by Miss Murray, was another property to be lost to the terminal along with other unoccupied former homesteads - Graves, Curries, Garson, Crowsnest, Upper House and Overhouse.

The remainder of the island is largely unaffected, except for alterations - usually improvements - in services like having a doctor, the ferry, electricity and water. Elf brought mains electricity to all the Flotta homes and upgraded the water supply. The South Isles ferry service runs several times a day, making it possible for islanders to take day trips to the Mainland, and for others to visit Flotta. The "Elf boat", available free of charge to Flotta residents, also operates a regular service to the Mainland. One custom has survived this 'improvement'. 'Before the oil' the ferry operated so infrequently that marriages had to be held on Fridays. There had been no crossing on a Sunday and a couple married on Saturday could not leave for a honeymoon until Monday. Despite the introduction of a Sunday crossing, Saturday weddings remain rare.

A special interlude and privilege during our stay on Flotta was to be invited by Bill Crichton, the Administration Superintendent, to look around the terminal. It was clear that we would have received the minimal or 'eleven-minute tour', if it hadn't been for the diary, our 'wacky' steps in following it here and our own enthusiasm for the adventure. Bill is also a character and when he arrived to meet us, he fired a few fierce questions as if to test our spirit. He tells a good story well, and didn't stop talking. After some teasing he didn't object to our recording his talk on our dictaphone, though he has never allowed it before. We said we didn't wish to "push our luck", but he laughed and replied good-naturedly that we already had.

In the classroom, we viewed aerial photographs of Flotta before, during and after the construction of the terminal, flow charts showing how all the processes work, and maps of all the Elf Group's oil fields and surface and submerged platforms in the North Sea. This terminal stabilises and ships crude oil from the complex of fields 130 miles offshore in the North Sea. Gas removed in the stabilisation is separated into Methane for driving the terminal and Ethane and Propane, also for shipment. The operation is not labour-intensive as the whole process is highly automated. Bill explained the process superbly, referring frequently to the colour-coded diagrams on the wall, which reminded us that he is an ex-schoolteacher.

It is often said that the flare must be a waste of gas, but in fact it is a safety valve. The main flare, so important to islanders as a symbol, is part of a system of three flares, the tallest being 220 feet high. When gas tankers arrive at the jetty, they too are connected to the flare system, like infants to the mother. Like the crude oil, the liquified gases are a valuable energy resource, and all these products - stable crude, Propane and Ethane - find a ready international market.

There are millions of gallons of water to be disposed of. For every barrel of oil from the older fields may come many barrels of salt water which must be processed just like oil. The treated water, though sampled, tested and approved for discharge, is not pumped into the sensitive waters of Scapa Flow. Rather it is pumped across the island to Kirk Bay and out by the island of Switha, the pipe running just below the Manse.

Great efforts are made not to affect or disturb the life of the islanders. If a problem arises the islanders are encouraged to make the terminal aware of it so that staff can respond quickly. On the way to Golta with Phyllis we had seen a ploughed field just outside the boundaries of the southern edge of the terminal. She explained that one day a man burnt off his heather field. Seeing the flames so near the tanks of liquid Propane gas, Elf's Loss Prevention Department had the field ploughed between the heather and the terminal as a fire break, and keep fire engines on stand-by when heather is alight. It is not their policy to tell the man not to burn his heather as this would be unwarranted interference.

Elf has worked in several ways to improve the economic prospects of Flotta and Orkney in general. Only a dozen or so of the 140 Flottarians work for Elf directly, but many carry out contract work to supplement their smallholdings. Bill claimed that over 90% of terminal employees are local people, but qualified this by saying that it depends on a wide definition of 'local'. Phyllis told us that Orkney's population is now less than half Orcadian, and we bore that in mind when Bill said that the Chief Engineer, for example, is 'from' Kirkwall.

The company had two objectives concerning its development on the island, aside from the financial one of doing good business. It would try to minimise damage to the environment and it would endeavour to employ local people. To that end, it helped those people who had reluctantly left Orkney in search of work to come home again, by offering assistance with re-location. Appreciating that not all of these people would or could live on Flotta, the daily passenger service was set up to ferry staff across Scapa Flow.

Bill concluded our fascinating afternoon at the terminal by presenting us with gifts: a copy of Thompson's History of Orkney, and of Armand Hammer's biography (the founder of the company), framed aerial photographs of Flotta, colour-illustrated copies of George Mackay Brown's *Portrait of Orkney,* and paperweights enclosing oil from the billionth barrel shipped out from the terminal in 1986.

Whether or not the terminal has seriously affected the island can be argued either way. Certainly it has changed island life. As Davick says "We have to look at our watches now". It matters more which day of the week it is. Flottarians cannot ignore it, and there are those who might claim that any alteration is bad. But, the island cannot be cocooned, and the islanders seem to have accepted the benefits while keeping a close eye on the smoke coming out of the flare.

When he observed that the Sunday morning fire practice was creating more black clouds than usual, Davick muttered about the 'unacceptable face of the oil industry' and Phyllis phoned Security to make them aware of it. Island life and terminal life go on in parallel, converging only at such points as the ferry, Phyllis and her family, and the ever-present symbol, the flare. The world inside the terminal is the world of telex, fax, computers and 84 inch pipes you could cycle along. It is the realm of national and international politics and is crucial to the British economy. It has produced one-fifth of Britain's oil and gas requirements for over fifteen years and there remain millions of barrels to be extracted. The rest of the island 'outwith' the wire fence is still the world of one man with ten jobs, of sheep, cattle, hay-making and lobster-fishing.

FAREWELL TO FLOTTA

On our last evening on Flotta, we stood in the Post Office talking to the Sinclairs and Rowland. Davick and Marina invited us into the house for a 'wee dram'. After this farewell toast, we shook hands and kissed cheeks. Flotta was now so familiar that we felt a part of it, sad at leaving and already thinking about when we would return. Having lived and learned a year's worth in just a few days, we were overwhelmed by the sense of welcome, good humour and happiness that radiated from our hosts. We left our mark in the Lairdy Visitors' Book:

Thanks to everyone for such a wonderful welcome and for so much help in researching the diary. We could not have hoped for a better visit.

To prove to the islanders that we were not taking all of their flora away in samples, we pressed a flower beside our entry.

In a daze of sleep and sadness, we rose at 5.30 a.m. Phyllis had gone to stay with Kenny for a week's holiday so we were alone. By 7 a.m., feeling desolate, we stood on the pier in the grey morning, thinking about the new friends we had made, and realising the truth of having to live one's own life rather than theirs.

Hoy wore its constant cap of cloud, and mist was hanging in the air. Fara and Cava were clear and distinct and Scapa Flow was flat calm. The flare was as vertical as we had seen it. A tanker was at one of the single point moorings, bow attached to it, and at its stern a tiny tug - all of Bill's teaching came to life.

ANTIQUITIES AND THE CREEL

On the Mainland, we hired a car for the day, costing 23 pounds from Peace's Garage, and headed straight for Skara Brae. Four coaches full of tourists were there ahead of us, the only other visitors we had encountered. The setting is beautiful, on the Bay of Skaill, with cliffs to either side and a horseshoe of pale sand. Skara Brae is the best-preserved pre-historic village in northern Europe. The huts were revealed in 1850 when a great storm tore away the dunes and grass which had covered them. Remarkable because their walls remain to full height, and flagstone furniture has stayed intact, we couldn't help but stare at the stone dressers, beds, boxes and seats which were all built and in use between 3000 and 2500 BC.

We drove on to the Ring of Brogar, a stone circle some 140 metres in diameter, in which 27 of the original 60 stones still stand. Dating from around 2500 BC and surrounded by a 10 metre-wide ditch cut into rock, the setting is dramatic with 360 degree views - fields of yellow flowers, distant mountains and boats on the shore of Loch Harray. A fine rain began to fall and we went on to the Stones of Stenness, another circle, where four of the twelve stones remain, the tallest over fifteen feet high. Unlike those at Brogar, or any others we have seen, these are sharp and angular in shape.

On to Maeshowe, and a chambered tomb from 2000 BC. It sits within a grassy mound one hundred feet across, and over twenty feet high. Bending double to enter by a three-feet high passage, in the inside darkness we heard a brief talk by the guide. On three sides are openings into the actual tomb chambers, and huge stones lying on the ground are the 'plugs' used to seal them.

The runic inscriptions fascinated us most. Left by the ransacking Vikings in the mid 12th century, the characters are delicate and artistic, finely carved into the stone walls with metal axes. One inscription says it was carved 'by the man who wrote the best runes in the western ocean', and another refers to Ingeborg, the Fair Widow, commenting that all women would have to lower themselves to enter there, whatever their airs and graces. On the shortest day in the year, the whole chamber is illuminated by the setting sun, which fills the tomb from an angle perfectly in line with a standing stone about a mile away, before it is left in darkness for another year.

From there, we drove across the four Churchill Barriers to St. Margaret's Hope on South Ronaldsay. Our guest house was a large double-fronted Georgian building overlooking the slipway in the small and charming fishing village. The interior was lovely with a sweeping staircase and plain wood doors, pictures, ornaments, cushions and rugs everywhere giving a wonderful air of artistic clutter. Our room was equally attractive. In the comfortable first floor lounge we drank coffee, read *The Orcadian* and wrote up our diaries, then departed for The Creel Restaurant.

The informal atmosphere was what we had come to expect and enjoy, and despite its excellent reputation, the surroundings are plain, simple and unpretentious. What matters here is the food. The Creel was runner-up in the Scottish Restaurant Competition in 1987. Some of the diners were dressed for a special occasion. Others, like us, were wearing trousers or jeans. The service was friendly and the waitress took time to explain the menu, leading us to be adventurous with our choices.

To start, 'Dressed Hunda Partan', local crab from Hunda, a small island off Burray (£2.75) and 'Terrine of the Creel', scallop, haddock, monkfish and leek terrine in vinaigrette (£2.40). The wine we chose was Alsace Gewurztraminer Reserve Speciale 1984 Paul Blanck (£8.75). For main course, 'Salmon St. Margaret's', salmon steak grilled, with scallops and prawns in garlic butter (£7.70) and 'Ronaldsvoe Chicken', breast of chicken stuffed with smoked salmon, poached in Noilly Prat with a light cream sauce

(£6.90). The food was even better than the menu descriptions suggested and arrived with Orkney 'tatties', crunchy courgettes and beetroot. This was *Nouveau Cuisine* in standard of presentation, but not in quantity. Eventually indulging in fresh strawberries and cream, and an amazing combination of chocolate mousse, meringue, creme caramel and cream, topped with a brandy snap, and then coffee and refills, it was a meal to be remembered, a celebratory event. Since we were nearing the end of our journey, we exchanged our diaries for the first time in a week, and engrossed ourselves in the other's observations. Nearly four hours after entering The Creel, we reluctantly left and walked home in the still night air.

17. Italian Chapel, Lamb Holm

SCAPA FLOW

Since Miss Murray's visit, Orkney has, of course, experienced two world wars. It is impossible to travel around present-day Orkney without being aware of the importance of its role, and that of its northerly cousin, Shetland, in defending the British Isles. Without relating here the historical events documented many times elsewhere, suffice it to say that Scapa Flow, the vast natural 'harbour' that separates the southern isles of Orkney, provided a haven for the British fleet.

Scars of war persist in the Flotta landscape, and it was through those that we learned of Orkney's war. From 1914, troops were stationed on Stanger Head and the King came to visit them two years later. Now rusting water tanks from World War II dominate this high point of the island and can be seen from afar. Driving around Golta, we saw bomb craters, ammunition stores, a derelict YMCA building and the garrison theatre, each indicating how different the island must have appeared during both wars, and all more of an interruption to Flotta's natural beauty than the oil terminal. Phyllis had showed us huge nets at Golta, still in position forty years after they were last dragged across Hoxa Sound to prevent German submarines penetrating Scapa Flow.

The now-famous Churchill Barriers were erected for the same reason. There are four in all, joining the small Orkney islands which skirt the eastern edge of Scapa Flow, with the Mainland. In October, 1939, on a foggy night with a particularly high tide, a German U-boat had slipped into Scapa Flow, past the sunken wrecks with which the entrances were supposedly blocked, to sink the Royal Oak, with the loss of over 800 men. The building of the barriers was a feat: a quarter of a million tons of stone and rock as foundations, topped with 66,000 concrete blocks weighing between five and ten tons each. The result is a total of one and a half miles of stone wall, in places submerged to a depth of over fifty feet, and constructed in spite of the added difficulty of strong tidal races between the islands.

The A961 road now runs across the top of each barrier, linking Lamb Holm, Glimps Holm, Burray and South Ronaldsay to the Mainland. The fifteen mile distance between South Ronaldsay, in the far south, and Kirkwall has thereby been reduced to a mere half-hour's drive. This accessibility is bemoaned by many. Before the war St. Margaret's Hope alone had over 20 shops but now only a handful remain. Phyllis' Aunt Lottie told us of the excitement in her mother's day of the annual event of a visit to Kirkwall, necessarily by boat, to buy a pig to fatten for Christmas. She remembered that her mother also returned with the latest gramophone records, which all their friends hurried round to hear.

When Churchill ordered the construction of the barriers, a large camp was set up to house Italian prisoners of war who were to undertake the work. These same prisoners created, on Lamb Holm, the renowned Italian Chapel. They longed for a place of worship of their own and in 1943, the Commandant and Chaplain acquiesced sympathetically. Two Nissen huts were placed end to end, and one prisoner, Domenico Chiocchetti, aided by fellow captives, transformed the interior with scrap metal, second hand wood and paint donated to them, into a place of exquisite beauty. A cement facade was added, and inside the whole was painted with *trompe l'oeuil* brickwork, dado rail and carved stone. Chiocchetti painted a Madonna and Child behind the altar and a superb ceiling to the nave. The whole concept of an ornate Italian chapel in the subdued Orkney landscape seemed incongruous to us and we expected it to be out of place and contrived, perhaps for the tourists, but definitely it is not. The fact that it is still so immaculately painted is purely that Chiocchetti has returned more than once to restore his work to its original glory, and it is genuine and moving in its appeal.

Now, of course, the deep waters of Scapa Flow can accommodate the largest oil tankers in the world.....

18. Italian Chapel ceiling, Lamb Holm

CYCLING ON SHAPINSAY

The day began at Kirkwall Harbour. We were going to explore Shapinsay, a small island north-east of the Mainland. As our ferry, a small Ro-Ro similar to the 'Hoy Head', docked, about 20 passengers disembarked for a day in the capital. A small cargo container was lowered onto the quayside and when the doors opened we were intrigued to see that the 'cargo' consisted of shopping trolleys, pushchairs and bicycles, which were then reclaimed by their respective owners. Once empty, it was re-filled and hoisted back onto the boat. Trays of peaches and apples were also loaded, presumably by request of the grocer on Shapinsay. We enjoyed thoroughly the half-hour trip on the 'Lyrawa Bay' and as we docked our first view was of Balfour Castle, built in 1848 by the owners of the island after whom the castle was named.

Strolling along the main street into Balfour village, we admired the estate workers' housing scheme, a single row of low, grey and russet stone cottages, directly fronting the road. Opposite each one, lying between the road and the water's edge, is an immaculately kept garden, and the whole scene of cottages, gardens, boats and islands is idyllic.

The Smithy is an old, weathered building with stone steps up the outside to first floor level, and it now houses museum, cafe and crafts shop. Parked outside was a very old tractor with wooden Hardy-esque cart. At the end of the row of cottages is a two-storey house, which is the Post Office, and in front of it a grey stone tower about ten feet high. As we approached, another grey tower came into view, and another two-storeyed house, the twin of the Post Office. The towers are entrance pillars, for between these and the two houses is a tree-lined unmade road leading to the castle.

Shapinsay's Post Office is also its general store, and offers car and bicycle hire. We paid £3.00 for two bicycles for the day, only to find they actually had only one bicycle left. We waited five minutes for one to be "borrowed from up the road" and this gave us the chance to look around. An entire wall of the small shop consisted of a bank of old biscuit tins, propped on their sides with transparent lids but containing modern packets of biscuits rather than loose ones as one might expect.

We studied the map and planned our route while sitting on a bench beside the waterfront gardens. The island is about eight miles long and six miles wide, maximum, but is shaped with a big bite out of the top. We set off and the first thing we encountered was a hill, but quickly getting into the swing of things, we cruised happily, reaching the church which was under renovation and without a roof. At the far end of the island is another, older stone building, also without a roof, but this is more a romantic ruin, set amongst long grasses and gravestones, overlooking the sea. We had learned that most Orcadian churches are sited next to the shore. It was easier to transport a coffin to the churchyard by sea for burial, and in more remote places, still is to this day.

Our cycles came to a screeching halt, when we saw a large patch of orchids and wild yellow iris. No samples of these for our pressed flower cards! At first we were unaware that some twenty cows in the adjacent field had all moved over to the fence to see what we were doing. Forty big brown eyes stare at us, and as we moved, all heads turned in unison. Further on is Mor Stein, a twelve foot standing stone, rendered so handsome by a thick covering of furry green-grey lichen that we stopped to take a closer look.

Re-mounting, we cycled in some discomfort along very rocky and stony farm tracks. All junctions are either cross-roads or T-junctions, as all the throughfares follow a strict grid pattern between the fields. We read that in the 1850s Lord Balfour revolutionised farming on the island, and one of his achievements was to divide the land into square ten acre fields bordered by straight roads.

On to Veantrow Bay. We were lured to the beach by promise of Odin's Stone, a giant pebble associated with Woden, but we could not identify it. Nevertheless, the coloured and patterned pebbles underfoot immediately captured our interest. We could not resist collecting a few more; pinks, greys, russets and blues, with very distinctive circular lines and swirls, and some appear inlaid. Sitting down to picnic, we attempted to identify the various islands spread before us: Gairsay, Rousay, Wyre, Eday, Westray and Egilsay. On the latter we could even see the hallowed St. Magnus church against the horizon and the whole view inspired us to call Shapinsay 'the gateway to the northern isles of Orkney'. The sea was mirror-smooth except for gentle ripples at the shore. We were facing due north yet the reflective light on the sea, on a dull day, was soft and constantly changing. 'Slivers' of island floated on the horizon.

Shapinsay seems much like Cornwall. Beautiful landscape, miles of coast, megalithic, insular, it seems as separate from Scotland as Cornwall is from England. These sentiments can be applied to Orkney as a whole. We wished to stay, but struggled back up the stony track to the road weighed down by our burden of pebbles. Free-wheeling down the long hill to Balfour village, it seemed a shame to battle up the hills only to come down again, but that's life.

Leaving our bicycles at the Post Office, we caught the last ferry (3.30 p.m.) by the narrowest margin. No time to visit the crafts shop and support the tourist industry. Once on the ferry, it was blustery but warm, and we realised that the cycling had given us a windburned glow. Back in Kirkwall, we made straight for the coffee shop - to drink coffee, of course, but more importantly to sort our pebbles. The table was covered and the waitress not amused, but after examining each pebble of the forty-six minutely, eight failed to justify the 1000 mile trip home. These we surreptitiously put back on a beach.

19. Italian Chapel altar, Lamb Holm

REFLECTIONS

We were in search of beautiful views and experiences, and we found them. Miss Murray wrote 'A Simple Diary of Orcadian Life'. We could not have done the same without ignoring a welter of detail that was at our fingertips. Orcadian life is no longer simple, but complicated by wars, television, cars, oil.....

Our questions, however, have been answered. We know the location of Flotta. We know it is still inhabited. There is a thriving community, though the only visitors, other than the islanders' relatives, appear to be eccentrics, or 'droll critters', like ourselves. Most tourists make for Hoy, by-passing Flotta, which in any case has no bed and breakfast accommodation.

Phyllis and her parents knew nothing about us at all, and yet welcomed us into their homes and their lives without hesitation or reservation. This was true of everyone we met in Orkney from the taxi-driver in Kirkwall who discovered our bus connections for us when we didn't know ourselves where to go, to the postman walking along the street who offered to take our parcels when the Post Office was closed. Unexpected service and kindness without exception.

Most of our adventure exceeded our expectations. A handful of Miss Murray's experiences - which we had hoped to recapture - eluded us. The Royal Hotel was a disappointment. The sun did not set at midnight and rise again at three o'clock, and there were no midnight fishing trips. Nonetheless, our entire visit was marked by a series of happy coincidences. Searching for bed and breakfast accommodation in Kirkwall, one lady who had no vacancies herself called a neighbour who housed us and this was Phyllis' Auntie Lottie. Our landlady from St. Margaret's Hope dined at The Creel

Restaurant on the same evening as we did, and always we seemed among friends.

Miss Murray was ever-present and we felt an empathy with that past. We felt closest to her on the train to Thurso, and on Flotta where we saw what she had seen. We treasured the experiences shared with her, staying at the Manse, walking to Lairdy, reading Crockett's *Lilac Sunbonnet*, and attending the church service. It was as if we travelled back in time. But, one glance at the flare and we were firmly back in the present. The oil industry cannot be ignored, but this is nevertheless a story of hope and optimism. Island life and spirit can exist alongside the invader.

Leaving Phyllis was strange and difficult, and words seemed hopelessly inadequate. She said goodbye when leaving the Manse for her week on the Mainland, leaving her home to us, but she also arranged to come and see us onto the St. Ola at Stromness. The next day we were hundreds of miles away.

Once home we attempted to analyse how the journey had changed our outlook. Aside from our samples of 'nature's gifts', we brought back with us memories, new ideas, new friends, and an absolute determination to return. It is seldom one reaches a milestone which is recognizable as such, but just as Flottarians regard the coming of oil as a landmark, referring to 'before' and 'after the oil', so we refer to 'before' and 'after-Orkney'. The tapestry of wonderful people - Phyllis, Marina, Davick, Hope, Mary, Bill....with countless others in supporting roles like Rowland, Kenny, Auntie Lottie - we have with us always. Our main lasting image must be the view from the Manse, overlooking Kirk Bay and the church and graveyard, with Mrs. Mitchell's white cross brilliant in the sunlight. Then evenings begun in the Post Office and concluded round the peat fire, and Mary reading from the diary and smiling in wonder.

This diary for us has many levels. It relates to Miss Murray's visit. It reflects the developing friendship between the two of us. It shows a slice of life on a small Orcadian island.

In a further 89 years' time it may fall into the hands of someone who again may retrace the patterns from 1900 to 1989 to 2078? If you are that person, we wish you luck and spur you on, because your adventure will be fulfilling and never to be forgotten.

20. Stromness scene

EPILOGUE

At the time of our visit to Orkney we knew very little about Miss Murray. Prior to setting out in July of 1989, we had advertised extensively in local newspapers in the Brechin and Aberdeen areas. Although we received only one reply, this was to yield valuable information. Miss Una Moffat of Brechin wrote that she had known Miss Murray's brother Fitz Roy, that their father had been a gun shop owner in the town and that Miss Murray had a poem, 'Glenesk' published in *A Glen Anthology*. With this information, the diarist emerged from the pages of the notebook and into reality: here was someone who knew of Miss Murray.

By correspondence with Miss Moffat we were able to confirm that Miss Murray's name was Brenda. After returning from our own 'mirror' journey to Flotta, we were able to obtain a copy of her birth certificate from the Edinburgh Records Office. This revealed to us that on visiting Orkney Brenda's age had been nineteen, much as we had gathered from the tone of her writing. She was born on 7 November 1880 in St. Andrew's Street, Brechin, to David Murray and Anna Maria Murray (nee Greig).

Having established her age, we could then instruct the Records Office to conduct a search over a five year period for a marriage certificate. From her 1951 postscript to the Orkney diary we knew that she became Mrs. Draper. In the first search nothing was revealed, and we repeated the request for the following five years. A copy certificate arrived from Edinburgh in January 1990; Brenda had married Thomas Andrew Draper on 29 April 1907 at her home, St. Katherine's, Castle Street, Brechin. The groom's address is given as The Poplars, 193 Newton Road, Burton upon Trent. Immediately we saw why all our letters and advertisements in Scotland had yielded such a dearth of information. It was also much more conceivable for a diary to show up in Gloucestershire from Burton, rather than from Scotland. At last we had made the English connection.

Within a few days we contacted the Burton Daily Mail to place an advertisement. Instead we found an interested reporter, Dave Stacey, who wrote up our story for his weekly 'The Mail Remembers' page. The response soon brought us closer to Brenda Murray Draper than we had dared hope. The impression we had gained from her Orkney diary was borne out by the many letters we received from Burton, which all spoke of a remarkable woman. The first was from Mrs. Lillie Smeaton, and prompted our immediate visit to Burton.

"I was very interested to read in the Burton Mail last evening about the Diary written by my very dear friend, Brenda Draper. She and her husband, Andrew, were contemporaries of my parents, my father working for the same firm, Bass & Co. Brewers. Brenda passed away in December 1962, aged 82, being the same age as my mother. I could give you quite a lot of information about both Brenda and Andrew

but it would be too much for me to write. I have so many happy memories of them both. I am 85 years old but the article in the Mail has given me a great deal to think about."

Our meeting with Lillie and her daughter, Mrs. Hilary Sutton, gave us a great deal to think about. For the first time we were face to face with close friends of Brenda, and heard her spoken of with much affection. Lillie reassured us that Brenda would not have minded our proposed publication. "She would have been delighted with what you're doing, and so would Andrew."

The Drapers appear to have been ahead of their time, early exponents of conservation, part of an intellectual set in Burton, and well-known figures about the town. The words of Mrs. Maisie Birch conjure up a striking image: "They were both tall and thin people - I believe I remember Mrs. Draper wearing a cloak."

In the late 1930s, the Drapers converted to vegetarianism, partly due to Brenda's ill health, as Andrew wrote in *Vegetarian News,*

"'God moves in a mysterious way His wonders to perform', and never shall I forget a momentous decision I was called upon to make on that first Sunday in November, 1937. Previously, a friend at a distance had posted to my wife some of the writings of the Rev. J. Todd Ferrier, founder of the Order of the Cross, in which she had become keenly interested, as the aims and ideals of the Fellowship profoundly appealed to her. One qualification for being a member was: <u>*Abstaining from hurting the creatures, eschewing bloodshed and flesh eating,*</u> <u>*and living upon the pure foods so abundantly provided by nature.*</u> *On that particular Sunday she had, unknown to me, written a letter to the Founder asking to be admitted as a Member of the Order and, as we keep nothing from each other, she handed me the letter to read, with the request that I should post it for her.*

Thinking of what all our relatives, friends, and the doctor would say if I acquiesced in such a proceeding, I begged of her to wait for one month while she tried the effects of going without meat, so the letter was laid aside until the evening. Then she startled me with the request: 'If you will post this, I will come to meet you on your return!' So overjoyed was I at the idea of her once more walking with me on the highway, that I dashed off to post without delay, and from that moment she became a vegetarian. Each day she added a few yards to her walks abroad, and made such a wonderful recovery that gradually she measured her distance by miles, no one being more astonished than our Doctor, whose remark was: 'It is a miracle for everyone to observe!'

Now I was in a further quandary, for we had the responsibility of our faithful maid, who had been with us many years, and we felt we could not compel her to change her diet. However, I suggested that she and I should have more meatless days during the week and, at the end of twelve months, after several further attacks of illness, I made up my mind definitely to become a Vegetarian. Our maid's reaction was summed up in the remark: 'I certainly shan't cook meat for myself!' Then, for a week or two, my wife had sleepless nights devising well-balanced, appetising, pure food menus, and I can most heartily say I've never enjoyed my food throughout my whole life anything like as much as I have since I burst the bubble of ignorance."

Hilary Sutton also produced the long-awaited photograph of Brenda, and an anthology of her poems, *The Dales of Derbyshire*, published in 1920. The photo is undated but undoubtedly an early one. To us she appears elegant, with strong features and cool beauty.

Our next call was on Harold Caulton of Winshill, Burton, who had addressed us with a letter full of detail.

"My parents had six children and although we lived two miles away, up a steep hill, Mrs. Draper regularly walked to see us kids - she had no children - we loved to hear her deep Scottish accent and the stories she told.

When I first left school, aged 13 in 1922, my job was butcher's errand boy; I took meat to Drapers' house and always received 1 penny from Mrs. Draper, that was good pocket money then. In later life the Drapers were strict vegetarians - so no more meat.

At 16 I was apprenticed to the building trade and joined my father later when I was a tradesman; we built up a good business as builders and funeral directors. I sold out 12 years ago as my wife died and I had no family to follow on. We did a lot of work for Drapers in those years and were even closer friends.

Mr. Thomas Andrew Draper worked for Bass, Ratcliffe and Gretton, the Burton Brewers, in their head office in Burton. Both were great gardeners, and I remember Andrew spending many hours at his portable typewriter writing articles for the press, etc.

They were a very devout couple and attended Anglican Church, they walked everywhere and both were slim and fit, always cheerful. Thomas Andrew Draper died on 14 January 1958 and was cremated at Markeaton Crematorium, Derby. The service was conducted by Miss K. Ruggins who was the leader of a religious community to which the Drapers belonged. She came from outside Burton because I had to send a car to Burton Station to collect her. I sent Mr. Draper's ashes to Messrs Black & Sons - Funeral Directors - Brechin, Angus, to be scattered by a stream where the couple had spent happy hours in earlier years. Robert Black had been given instructions earlier about the scattering.

Brenda Murray Draper died on 5 December 1962 and her funeral arrangements were exactly as her husband's - Miss K. Ruggins again officiating. I have a feeling she was from the Cheltenham area. Mrs. Draper's ashes were scattered with Andrew's.

I personally arranged and conducted both funerals, a service they both asked me to perform.

Mrs. Draper left my nephew - who was only a small child when she died - an oil painting of a boy, which he still treasures. She was a great friend to us all.

I enclose a letter she sent to me for one of my Council Elections as she was one of my most ardent supporters. I only wish she could have lived until I was Mayor of the County Borough of Burton or when I was first Chairman of East Staffs District Council after local government re-organisation - she should have written many things."

Brenda's letter to Harold Caulton is dated May, 1961 and reads:

"Dear Harold,
If by putting a bigger X! or marking in 3 I could 'put you in' - I would! Your address to electors is the best I've seen. I know Andrew would have been delighted with its true straightforward tone - as I am. I am sure there will be no difficulty on Thursday. You have given of your best - and for the Common weal - no rash promises.
My brother has gone north again but what his visit has meant to me - I would have liked you to have met - but you are so occupied - 22 years is a long time & so much has happened.
My love to your Mother and to Mary - so glad when George told me of her 'runs' in the car.
Good fortune at the Polls!"

Harold gave us a real flavour of the era, describing Brenda as "a tall, sedate Edwardian lady". She always asked to see the children, who were taught to treat her with great respect. Rose was "a maid in the days of long white ribbons down her back" and Brenda "never lost her Scottish accent - she never intended to! - and her terrific laugh could be heard all over the house." On calling at the Drapers' a visitor may have been offered a cup of hot lettuce tea - "not always palatable, but you drank it!" As he discussed Brenda's house and their way of life, how they walked miles to church and how she laughed, Harold provided us with insights that we could not have found with anyone else. He returned the compliment by commenting, "You have stirred us all up. We've talked about someone we'd talked of a lot in life but not talked about, though thought of, for twenty years. It's brought someone back we'd lost."

We had written a letter to the occupants of the Drapers' old home at 193 Newton Road, Burton, and received a warm welcome from Mrs. Val French. The house is imposing, standing in a terraced garden high above the road, with views over the River Trent. Clearly fascinated by the history of her home, Mrs. French brought out a box of old documents. One was an Agreement signed in 1865 by Thomas Wilkins Draper, Andrew's grandfather, who was therein commissioning a local builder to construct the house for the family.

Many original features from Brenda's day were deliberately retained by Mr. and Mrs. French and adapted as part of their home. The safe, which has large keys with safety rods, now provides kitchen storage. The wash-house in the back garden is also well preserved, complete with copper, and a cabinet for fire beneath. So well known had been the Drapers' and Rose's collective enthusiasm for their garden, that Val French has continued to tend and maintain their plants. Harold Caulton described them as "meticulous gardeners" and Andrew Draper's diary catalogued each crop, its sowing and harvesting and its different varieties. He also described how they "always left half a dozen good pears at the top of the tree, for the birds, and to ensure good luck with next year's crop."

Upon Brenda's death in 1962, the house and contents were left to Rose, who maintained everything entirely unchanged. Val French was a friend of Rose, and could therefore describe how Rose continued to treat the house as belonging to the Drapers rather than as her own. She left all their diaries, correspondence and photographs in their desks and cupboards. In 1986, when Rose died, a part of the Drapers' effects were disposed of when a dealer removed some furniture and papers. Thus the 1900 Orkney diary ended up in the second-hand bookshop in Gloucestershire in the following year.

In the possession of Geoffrey Thursfield, a local historian, were two more of Brenda's diaries from the 1920s. Generously he was prepared to lend them to us, and through these we came to know her even better. The diaries cover the period 1923-27 and are both entitled *Nature Notes and Ornithological Observations*. They are written in the same beautiful hand, and contain equally vivid descriptions of bird life, flora and walks in the country surrounding Burton. Recounting journeys much further afield, Brenda told of holidays in Switzerland, France, the Cotswolds, Devon and Cornwall. More paths for us to retrace?

ACKNOWLEDGEMENTS

We would especially like to thank the following for their help towards our project: Alan Green, Phyllis Sinclair, David and Marina Sinclair, Bill Crichton and the Elf Enterprise Consortium (Elf Enterprise, Texaco, Lasmo, Union Texas), Mary Fortnum, Catherine McDonald and Donald Gillies, Angus Findlater and Ken Ross, Rowland Hill Barnett, Hope Sinclair, Kenny Gee, Charlotte Omand, Mr. and Mrs. Sulat, Una Moffat, Arunda and Ken Peters, Derek Tangye, Edinburgh Records Office, The *Brechin Advertiser, Kirriemuir Herald, Aberdeen Press and Journal, Mearn's Leader (Stonehaven),* Ian Gilmour, and our friends and families especially Malcolm Sutton, Michael McEwan, our parents and Martin Buxton.

Ten percent of the proceeds from sales of this book will be donated to Orkney Seal Rescue and Flotta Church Fabric Fund. *The Orkney Chronicles* is published with the generous assistance of the following to whom we are most grateful:

SPONSORS

L. I. Brown
Martin Buxton
Elf Enterprise Consortium
John English
Alan, Linda, Russell, Alex and Katie Green
Jacksons Financial Services - a member of the Jacksons Insurance Group
Orkney Islands Council
Barbara and Bob Parker
Martin R. Parker
Mr. C.S. and Mrs. J. Ringrose
Phyllis Sinclair
Lillie E. Smeaton
Malcolm D. Sutton
Edwina and Donald Witts

SUBSCRIBERS

Josh Adams and Jane Mitchell
Mr. and Mrs. L. J. Anderson
Mr. and Mrs. B. Baughan
Paula Brown
Robin and Penny Burnett
C. and B.M. Buxton
Harold Caulton
Kathleen Joan Cecil
Jacquie and Michael Cole
Andrew Collins
Martin Crosfill
Cathy Curran
Claire Dandridge
Fiona de Quidt
Sheila Duffy
Barrie Edwards
David Edwards
Mrs. E. V. English
Alison and Jonathan Etchells
Nigel and Mary Hallard
John Healy
Keith Hooper
Dr. Anthony Hughes
Mrs. E.M. Hughes
Lucille Johns
S.A. and D.P. Judd
Anne Lacey and Kevin Winship
June Lander
Alethea and Rodney Laredo
Lydia Meadows
Peggy Morris
Mrs. Angela Norman
Andrew, Sonia and Kate Newcombe
Mr. and Mrs. A.M. Newton

William R. Parker
Mrs. K.L. Parnham
Glenyse Pulford
Nigel Puttick
George Walton Scott
Diana Shears
Beryl and Brian Smith
Jane Squire
Kevin and Denise Stone
Hilary Sutton
Robert A. Sutton
Dee Tabb
D. Theed
Jill Tregunna
Roger Venables
Tom Waters
Chris Whitehall
Lauren Wright
and others who wish to remain anonymous.

A page for your notes

A page for your notes

A page for your notes